"Donna-Marie Cooper O'Boyle has the great ability to speak to and spiritually connect with the hearts of her readers."

Doug Keck
Host of *EWTN Bookmark*

"Offers Donna-Marie's unique brand of encouragement and spiritual guidance, amazing anecdotes of a life well lived, plus reflection questions, prayers, and more to help you know, love, and serve God more fully every day."

Lisa M. Hendey
Author of *A Book of Saints for Catholic Moms*

"Whether you are single or married, managing a busy household buzzing with children or adjusting to the quiet of an empty nest, *Rooted in Love* will give you the spiritual inspiration and practical tools you need to embrace your calling as a Catholic woman."

Mary DeTurris Poust
Author of *Cravings: A Catholic Wrestles with Food, Self-Image, and God*

"Brings common sense back to the table! Donna-Marie's practical wisdom helps women to see their lofty vocation, but in a down-to-earth way."

Rev. Leo Patalinghug
Author of *Grace before Meals*

"Count on Donna-Marie to affirm, encourage, enlighten, and edify. *Rooted in Love* explores the foundational truth that our calling as Catholic women is to discover who we are in Christ, and subsequently to become the disciples we are meant to be."

Karen Edmisten
Author of *After Miscarriage*

"A wonderful book for every Catholic woman. Beautiful and inviting, it is solid, balanced, and practical. I especially loved the many stories Donna-Marie tells of Christian love in action and of how God gave her strength to endure her own crosses."

Ronda Chervin
Coauthor of *What The Saints Said About Heaven*

ROOTED in LOVE

Our *Calling* as
Catholic
Women

DONNA-MARIE COOPER O'BOYLE

ave maria press AMP notre dame, indiana

Founded in 1865, Ave Maria Press is a ministry of the United States Province of Holy Cross.

www.avemariapress.com

Paperback: ISBN-10 1-59471-306-5, ISBN-13 978-1-59471-306-4

E-book: ISBN-10 1-59471-355-3, ISBN-13 978-1-59471-355-2

Cover image © plainpicture/Scheller.

Cover and text design by Katherine Robinson Coleman.

Printed and bound in the United States of America.

Library of Congress Cataloging-in-Publication Data

O'Boyle, Donna-Marie Cooper.

 Rooted in love : our calling as Catholic women / Donna-Marie Cooper O'Boyle.

   p. cm.

 ISBN 978-1-59471-306-4 (pbk.) -- ISBN 1-59471-306-5 (pbk.)

 1. Catholic women--Religious life. 2. Christian life--Catholic authors. I. Title.

 BX2353.O27 2012

 248.8'43--dc23

                               2012025592

Lovingly,

for my children:

Justin, Chaldea,

Jessica, Joseph, and

Mary-Catherine.

And for my

dear sister

Barbara

who was just called

home to heaven.

CONTENTS

ACKNOWLEDGMENTS

With a grateful heart to all the amazing women in my life: Thank you for your guidance and love and for accompanying me on the journey!

To my mother, Alexandra Mary Uzwiak Cooper, for bringing me into this world against doctor's orders, and for lovingly teaching me to give without counting the cost. To my grandmother, Alexandra Theresa Karasiewicz Uzwiak, for her inexhaustible love, guidance, and inspiration. To my godmother, Aunt Bertha Uzwiak Barosky, for her love and contagious optimism. To my Aunt Mary Uzwiak Buchman for the special love imparted to me as I grew up. To my three daughters, Chaldea, Jessica, and Mary-Catherine, in thanksgiving for their love and blessing in my life. To my sisters, Alice Jean Cooper Doriocourt and Barbara Janet Cooper Schonert, for their sisterly love.

To my other mother, friend, and mentor, dear Blessed Mother Teresa, with deep thanks for her selfless lessons of love imparted to me and her continued guidance and prayers from heaven. To dear Mother Mary, our Blessed Mother, for mothering me, for protecting me, and for forever being my saving grace!

A warm thanks to all who have guided me, prayed for me, and loved me throughout my life, my family and friends, especially my parents, Eugene Joseph and Alexandra Mary Uzwiak Cooper, and my brothers and sisters: Alice Jean, Gene, Gary, Barbara, Tim, Michael, and David. With grateful thanks to my friend and spiritual guide Father Bill C. Smith for his love and continual guidance and my friend, spiritual guide, and my daughter's godfather Servant of God Father John A. Hardon, S.J., for his marvelous wisdom and continued prayers and guidance from heaven. I am eternally indebted to all.

My children have always been my utmost vocation and life. I love you Justin, Chaldea, Jessica, Joseph, and Mary-Catherine! My husband, David, the wind beneath my wings, thank you for your love and support! Heartfelt thanks to Robert Hamma, Thomas Grady, and the wonderful team at Ave Maria Press for their partnership in getting this book out to you. Lastly, with heartfelt gratefulness and loving prayers for all who are connected with me through my books and talks. Thank you for joining me on the journey that leads to LIFE. God bless you all!

INTRODUCTION

> All is vanity except knowing, loving and
> serving God. This alone can bring peace to
> my soul.
>
> —St. Katherine Marie Drexel

Today's Catholic woman need not feel alone or discouraged.
There is an amazing richness to the Catholic faith that can be
unearthed and applied to our lives. Catholic womanhood is
steeped in tremendous love, transforming grace, and fulfill-
ing joy. Our mission and vocation are rooted in love of God,
who actually stoops down to serve us, his creatures, even as
we strive to serve him. Amazing!

The Catholic Church upholds the dignity of women. We
learn about that affirmation in many Church documents,
including *Mulieris Dignitatem* (*On the Dignity and Vocation of
Women*). Blessed John Paul II bolstered us in our sublime role
and reminded us that "the witness and the achievements of
Christian women have had a significant impact on the life
of the Church as well as of society" (*MD* 27).

In our time, more than ever before, Catholic women are
pressing forward, moving deeper into their faith, and feeling
more recognized as an integral part of the Church. Blessed
John Paul II said,

In our own days too, the Church is constantly enriched
by the witness of the many women who fulfill their vocation to holiness. Holy women are an incarnation of the
feminine ideal; they are also a model for all Christians,
a model of the "*sequela Christi*" [followers of Christ], an
example of how the Bride must respond with love of the
Bridegroom." (*MD* 27)

How do we enrich our Church and fulfill our womanly
vocation to holiness? And how can Catholic women make
a significant impact on the life of the Church as well as on
society as Blessed John Paul II suggests? I feel quite certain
that I learned the answer to these seemingly unapproachable
questions in first grade!

I am dating myself, but I vividly remember sitting at
my little desk at St. Mary's school and Sister Mary Therese
asking the class, "Why did God make you?" In unison we
answered, "God made me to know him, to love him, and to
serve him in this world, and to be happy with him forever
in the next." This, of course, is straight out of the old *Balti-
more Catechism*. Even though many today are too young to
remember it, its age-old words of wisdom can resound in
our hearts today. They are the answer we are looking for,
the absolute key to our eternal happiness!

Of course, knowing, loving, and serving God is not
always easy. I've been through many difficulties in my life,
and I'm sure there will be more. I know what it's like to be in
foreclosure and worried about how I will provide a roof over
my children's heads. I intimately know the pain of divorce
and what it's like to be a single mother for many years. I've
been falsely accused. I've lost three of my babies to miscarriage. I've been physically assaulted (more than once). As
a single mother, I had to bail my son out of jail after he was

carted off in handcuffs from our home (for a crime he did not commit) while his younger sister watched helplessly.

I've lost both of my parents, my brother Gary, and my sister Barbara. I almost died during surgery. I've been in a terrible car accident that left me with permanent injuries and ongoing pain. I've felt stretched beyond measure to try to keep up with responsibilities. I've suffered with serious illness. There's more, but my point in listing some of my struggles is to assure you that I'm right here with you in knowing what the pain feels like and just how the uncertainties regarding the multitude of challenges can tug at your heart and twist your brain. Throughout this book, I'll share a few of my own grueling experiences and try to offer some hope and suggestions on what it means for us as Catholic women to know, love, and serve God in this world, even in the face of trouble and hardship.

I treasure the simple yet profound words from a beloved woman, St. Clare of Assisi, who said, "Love God, serve God: everything is in that."[1] Throughout this book we will explore how we can live an amazingly meaningful and happy life as we comes to know, love, and serve God with our feminine mind, heart, and hands. We will also draw from solid Church resources including the *Catechism of the Catholic Church* and other recent teachings of both Pope Benedict XVI and Blessed John Paul II. I speak often about Blessed Teresa of Calcutta and the Jesuit scholar Servant of God John A. Hardon, S.J. That's because I knew both of them personally, and Father Hardon was for a time my spiritual director. I want to share the blessings I was privileged to receive through them.

After each chapter I will provide reflection questions so that you can ponder some suggested ways in which to know God better, to love him more, and to serve him always.

The book can also be used in a group study by reading each chapter together and then reflecting on the suggested points to ponder found at the end of each chapter. When women get together—watch out! We have the power, by God's grace, to change the world. This can occur—one soul at a time—through faithful women's influence and in larger ways, too. We'll look at this in more depth throughout the book.

One time I gave a talk to a lovely group of women in New York who told me that they'd love to extend my presentation by having a sleepover party with me. Of course, they were joking. Well, really only half joking. It was such a sweet response and affirmation to my lecture. I would have loved to stay with them, too—they were delightful. It reminded me that we women love to keep company with one another and share our faith. But oftentimes we lack the time and the opportunity to do so.

Let's have our own "slumber party" throughout this book and endeavor to discover that "everything" St. Clare expressed. Let's celebrate our Catholic womanhood!

PART ONE

*D*ISCOVERING MYSELF IN CHRIST

A woman's dignity is closely connected with the
love which she receives by the very reason of her
femininity; it is likewise connected with the love
she gives in return.

—*Mulieris Dignitatem* 29

1. WHO AM I?

In God's eternal plan, woman is the one in
whom the order of love in the created world
of persons takes first root.

—*Mulieris Dignitatem 29*

On a cold but bright and sunny winter day, I was dressed
in a frilly beautiful gown, satin shoes, and lacy socks—all
in white, swaddled in a blanket, and driven to the church,
I was quite a bundle—weighing in at a pleasantly plump
ten pounds twenty-five days earlier at my birth. I know all
of this because I have seen the photos and have been given
the details. My parents, Eugene and Alexandra Cooper, and
my godparents, Alfred Uzwiak and Bertha Barosky, atten-
tively participated and spoke on my behalf so that I could
enter the Church when the baptismal waters flowed over my
head on December 18, 1955, at St. Mary Church in Stamford,
Connecticut.

I was told I didn't cry at all, and it makes me happy to
know that I was completely content during that sacramental celebration. Quite possibly there wasn't a peep out of
me because my little tummy was full and I was sleeping
away! My grandmother, Alexandra Uzwiak, was present,

too, as were many other relatives and my six older siblings, all congregating around the baptismal font, with some up on their tiptoes to watch. Afterward, they all gathered for a big party to celebrate my becoming an "official" Catholic at our home on Lockwood Avenue.

BEGINNING WITH OUR BAPTISMS

You know, we're not Catholic because we know about the faith or even because we live the faith and participate in the Catholic Church by going to Mass. We are Catholic first and foremost because we were baptized. Baptism is a big deal! It's not merely a nice tradition. It's a sacrament that initiates us into the big Church with a capital "C." Being baptized a Catholic is truly extraordinary. While most of us remember absolutely nothing about it since we were tiny babes when we experienced it, what actually happened to us at the moment of Baptism is indeed well worth pondering now. And those of us who were baptized as adolescents or adult have a wonderful story to share with the rest of us.

Baptism is truly a gateway to life in the Spirit, a *"vitae spiritualis ianua,"* the *Catechism* says (CCC 1213). Baptism frees us from sin and opens the gate to the other sacraments as it identifies us as true members of Christ, incorporating us into the Church. St. Gregory of Nazianzus superbly described the sacrament. He said,

> Baptism is God's most beautiful and magnificent gift. . . .
> We call it gift, grace, anointing, enlightenment, garment
> of immorality, bath of rebirth, seal, and most precious
> gift. It is called *gift* because it is conferred on those who
> bring nothing of their own; *grace* since it is given even
> to the guilty; *Baptism* because sin is buried in the water;
> *anointing* for it is priestly and royal as are those who are
> anointed; *enlightenment* because it radiates light; *clothing*

since it veils our shame, *bath* because it washes; and *seal*
as it is our guard and the sign of God's Lordship. (CCC
1216)

Pope Benedict XVI has said, "Heaven opens above us in
the sacrament of baptism. The more we live in contact with
Jesus in the reality of our baptism, the more heaven will
open above us" (homily, January 7, 2007). Baptism begins
with signing the child with the Cross, signifying the grace
of redemption won by Christ. Prayers of exorcism are said,
freeing us from the power of sin and the evil one. Baptism
is such a vital sacrament, such a powerful sacrament. It for-
gives all sins (original and personal) as well as all punishment for sin.

The sacrament imparts sanctifying grace on us that
gives us supernatural life and opens us to the Holy Trinity.
It indelibly marks us, very much like a brand to our soul,
and because it does, it cannot be repeated. It never leaves
us, even if we were to lose our faith. The waters of Baptism,
as well as the holy chrism (perfumed oil consecrated by the
bishop), used to anoint us when baptized, and the words by
the priest bring us fully into the Church. Through Baptism,
we permanently "put on Christ" through the Holy Spirit.
And without this basic sacrament we are not able to receive
any of the other six remaining sacraments.

Jesus himself, to set an example for us, submitted to Baptism by John, even though it was intended for sinners. He
also instituted the sacrament of Baptism by commanding
his disciples to proclaim the Gospel to all nations and to
baptize them (Mt 28:19).

Blessed Mother Teresa knew without a doubt that Baptism was an amazing sacrament that could bring someone
straight to heaven. She ministered to the sick and dying in
Calcutta, India, and other places as well. She offered the

dying what she notoriously called a "ticket to heaven."
She never pushed the life-transforming sacrament on anyone, but she asked each of them if they would like it before
closing their eyes on this earthly life. She said no one has
refused, and because of this we can imagine she has popu-
lated heaven with countless souls!

My mother, who weighed only a mere pound and a half
at birth (at a time when incubators weren't readily available), wasn't dressed as stylishly on her baptismal day as I
was for mine because she was immediately baptized in the
hospital on the day she was born. I'm sure she was simply
swaddled in her hospital blanket and the attending hospital chaplain did the honors of bringing her swiftly into the
Church through the waters of Baptism. My grandmother
didn't want to take the chance of my mother dying without
the precious sacrament. Although our Lord is certainly merciful, my grandmother wanted to be sure my mother would
make it to heaven safely.

The cardboard shoebox, cotton, and hot water bottle that
kept my mother's wee body warm and safe really saved her
life—that and, of course, her mother's attentive love, care,
and prayers. At the hospital, when the baptismal waters
were poured over my mother, Alexandra's, tiny head, she
became a member of the Body of Christ, a sharer in the life of
the Trinity. Thanks be to God my mother not only survived
her miniscule birth weight but also grew up to marry and
have eight children of her own.

My former spiritual director and dear friend (now
deceased) Father Bill C. Smith preached that our baptismal
certificates should be framed and prominently displayed in
our homes. He said that our baptismal day in his opinion
was especially important to celebrate, even more important
than our birthday. So, perhaps it's time to get those certificates out, dust them off, and hang them up! If you are a

mother or grandmother, frame each of your children's and grandchildren's certificates and hang them in their bedrooms or even in a common area of your home. Then you will be more aware of which special dates to celebrate. You can contact the parish where your child or children were baptized to get a fresh copy of the certificate complete with the parish's official imprinted seal.

My baptismal certificate is displayed in a lovely white frame in my bedroom, a constant reminder to me of that beautiful holy occasion. I make a point of pondering, praying, and meditating on the anniversary of my Baptism and asking our Lord to shower me with many graces on the remembrance of that pivotal day. Each family member's baptismal anniversary is a great reason to rejoice. Make a nice dinner or dessert, light a candle, make it special, and thank God for the blessing of becoming a child of his and an honored member in the Catholic Church.

During the last Angelus message of Christmas season 2011–2012, Pope Benedict XVI said, "Baptism is a new birth that precedes our actions. With our faith we can go to meet Christ, but only he can make us Christian and give to our will, to our desire, the answer, the dignity, the power to become children of God." He closed with a prayer to the Blessed Mother reminding us all that after being baptized we should demonstrate who we are in words and deeds. "To the Virgin Mary, Mother of Christ and all who believe in him, we ask you to help us truly live as children of God not with words, or not only with words, but with deeds" (January 9, 2012). How we can live out our Christian life in deeds is what we'll be exploring throughout this book.

Your Dignity as a Woman

Somewhere beneath the surface of our lives exists an incredible God-given and magnificent dignity as a woman. I say that it's hidden because, for many women, when they recognize their true dignity, it is a sheer delight, perhaps even an unexpected surprise. Women have contended with incredible hardship throughout the centuries in a myriad of ways. Women have been discriminated against and pushed to the margins of society throughout history. Because of this, many women have had great difficulties holding their heads up high during all sorts of circumstances, experiencing low self-worth, feeling inferior to men, or just not feeling up to their divine calling as a woman.

When explaining Jesus' great love for women, in his *Letter to Women*, Blessed John Paul II wrote, "[Christ] honored the dignity which women have always possessed according to God's plan and in his love."[1] The key words here about our dignity in God's eyes are "always possessed." I'll discuss this in greater depth, but for now, let's look at some of the problems and origins of the confusion about women's dignity.

The world tries to push a false identity on women based on its corrupt values. Most of that comes to us through an onslaught of messages via the mass media and the culture, which is hard to escape. This naturally creates a kind of tension between God and the world with which women are forced to contend.

As we know, the sexual revolution and radical feminism of the sixties occurred in part because women revolted and wanted to embrace the same rights as men. Most of them simply wanted to free themselves from the shackles of perpetual abuse, but it unfortunately backfired on women.

Women felt compelled to embrace a very lopsided version of womanhood. Droves of women bought into the notion of radical feminism and ferociously pursued the work force, leaving their young children behind in day-care centers while trying to prove their worth to the world. Women became progressively more depressed, many developing eating disorders. The family unit began to crumble. Pornography encroached insidiously upon family life, and the divorce rate skyrocketed as women became increasingly objectified. Human life was no longer regarded as precious and unrepeatable while countless abortions were performed to the tune of millions of dollars in blood money lining abortionist's pockets, under the deceptive guise of freedom of choice.

Before all of this happened, in 1968, Pope Paul VI prophetically outlined a warning in his encyclical *Humanae Vitae* (*On Human Life*). He pointed to the potential dangers ahead if society continued to accept a contraceptive mentality stemming from radical feminism and the sexual revolution in which abortion and contraception were viewed as rights and freedoms. He said,

> Let us first consider how easily this course of action could open wide the way for marital infidelity and a general lowering of moral standards. Not much experience is needed to be fully aware of human weakness and to understand that human beings—and especially the young, who are exposed to temptation—need incentives to keep the moral law, and it is an evil thing to make it easy for them to break that law. Another effect that gives cause for alarm is that man who grows accustomed to the use of contraceptive methods may forget the reverence due to a woman, and, disregarding her physical and emotional equilibrium, reduce her to being a mere

> instrument for the satisfaction of his own desires, no longer considering her as his partner whom he should surround with care and affection. (HV 17)

Those rights and freedoms that women were aggressively running after are the very things that have objectified them. And lest you think I am all gloom and doom, I'll remind you of what I said a bit earlier: *Somewhere beneath the surface of our lives exists an incredible God-given and magnificent dignity as a woman.* I'd like to suggest that the solution to the problems of objectification, exploitation, and mass confusion aimed at women is to earnestly and prayerfully seek to discover our true dignity as women, reveal it with great joy, and then do our part to assist other women to unearth their true God-given dignity.

But where do we possibly begin? I personally find it very comforting and healing to take to heart poignant words of wisdom from our Church, specifically Blessed John Paul II 's brilliant and tender words in *Mulieris Dignitatem* and in his *Letter to Women*. In this letter he lamented and even openly apologized for the serious evils of inequality, oppression, discrimination, and exploitation of women. He knew that the ill treatment of women throughout the centuries was not Jesus' way. He was well aware of women's lofty dignity and expressed it so eloquently while also pointing out the remarkable work of women and their indispensable significance in salvation history.

I have personally seen many women turn misty-eyed upon hearing about their own God-given dignity through our former pontiff's honest, forthright, and tender words:

> Women's dignity has often been unacknowledged and their prerogatives misrepresented; they have often been relegated to the margins of society and even reduced to servitude. This has prevented women from truly being

themselves and it has resulted in a spiritual impov-
erishment of humanity. Certainly it is no easy task to
assign blame for this, considering the many kinds of
cultural conditioning which down the centuries have
shaped ways of thinking and acting. And if objective
blame, especially in particular historical contexts, has
belonged to not just a few members of the Church, for
this I am truly sorry. May this regret be transformed,
on the part of the whole Church, into a renewed com-
mitment of fidelity to the Gospel vision. When it comes
to setting women free from every kind of exploitation
and domination, the Gospel contains an ever relevant
message which goes back to the attitude of Jesus Christ
himself. Transcending the established norms of his own
culture, Jesus treated women with openness, respect,
acceptance and tenderness. In this way he honored the
dignity which women have always possessed according
to God's plan and in his love. As we look to Christ at
the end of this Second Millennium, it is natural to ask
ourselves: how much of his message has been heard and
acted upon? (*Letter to Women*)

Isn't it nice to learn of such affirming words from our
Church? We should prayerfully ask ourselves the question
that Blessed John Paul II posed: how much of Christ's message has been heard and acted upon? It would appear that
not all that much has been heard or acted upon. In addition to discrimination, exploitation, and objectification of
women, there are all kinds of mixed messages from our
culture and the mass media targeted at women that cause us
confusion and discouragement. Many women feel a need to
satisfy society's expectations for perfection, whether it is in
their appearances, lifestyles, or whatever else. It's no secret
that women are bombarded. And we can become conditioned by society's standards, rather than searching deeper

in our hearts and looking up as well, to ponder what God expects of us. I write and speak a lot about this predicament that women find themselves caught in. Many women in my audiences tell me afterward that the sheer acknowledgment of women's challenges helps them feel affirmed in their plight and also helps them to recognize areas to keep an eye on and how they can prayerfully confront the problems.

Even though we might feel surrounded by negativity, discouragement, and a false perception of what an authentic woman should be like, I believe that today there is a huge resurgence of folks all over getting deeper into their faith to learn the Truth, particularly women. Women are inclined to share their hearts and are getting together in a cyber way and in the flesh to learn more about their faith and to share their insights with other women.

God gives women specific gifts in her role as a daughter, wife, mother, sister, niece, aunt, grandmother, single woman, widow, and consecrated religious. Not that we need to get a big ego, but I think it's nice to be reminded every once in a while—women have been given gifts to be heroic, strong, loving, nurturing, instructive, protective, encouraging. . . . The list goes on and on. Are we tapping into our God-given gifts? Do we use them?

I love what Servant of God Archbishop Fulton Sheen (whose cause for beatification has begun) has expressed about a woman's power. Although he was speaking about the love of a man and a woman, the last line is the clincher:

> When a man loves a woman, he has to become worthy of her. The higher her virtue, the more noble her character, the more devoted she is to truth, justice, goodness, the more a man has to aspire to be worthy of her. The history of civilization could actually be written in terms of the level of its women.[2]

Imagine that!

He gives us some beneficial food for thought. We really should ponder the level of our own personal virtues and our devotion to the Truth. If we're mediocre in those areas, so will our society be. If we are immoral in those areas, well, we are dragging society down the tubes. I think you get the picture. We have to wake up and recognize that we as women truly have the power to get things moving in the right direction.

I Belong

When we are growing up, invariably, we are asked, "What do you want to be when you grow up?" We usually have all kinds of hopes and dreams about the future, some perhaps crazy, some optimistic. I remember one time when I was sorting through boxes of family memorabilia and old school papers, I came across an illustration created by my oldest son, Justin, complete with his bold exuberant statement, "When I grow up I want to be a scientist!" I can imagine him gleefully putting his heart into his creation as he scrawled out his declaration in his best penmanship.

Well, I had forgotten all about that young desire of his, but I was glad to come across it that day. It caused me to pause a moment amid boxes of stuff and reflect on little Justin's dream. Justin, now thirty-five, was and is, no doubt, a very brilliant guy. But he never did pursue the sciences; rather, he is involved in technology, music, and the arts.

St. Thérèse of Lisieux boldly exclaimed, "At last I have found my vocation. My vocation is love."[3] "Vocation" comes from a Latin word that means "calling." The primary vocation of every person is holiness and the perfection of love. Whatever state of life we find ourselves in as Catholic

women—married, single, mother, or consecrated religious—
each one requires our ascent to holiness and love.

Blessed John Paul II has said,

> In the hidden recesses of the human heart the grace of
> a vocation takes the form of a dialogue. It is a dialogue
> between Christ and an individual, in which a personal
> invitation is given. Christ calls the person by name and
> says: "Come, follow me." This call, this mysterious
> inner voice of Christ, is heard most clearly in silence
> and prayer. Its acceptance is an act of faith." (homily,
> February 10, 1986)

Perhaps a question we might ask ourselves somewhere
along our faith journey is, "How and when do I *hear* my
personal and specific calling from God regarding what I
should do with my life?" St. Teresa of Avila said she prac-
tically forced herself to become a nun because she knew
it would be good for her. The manner in which one hears
one's personal call certainly varies as the years go by. When
younger, we might ask ourselves, "Should I marry? Should
I pursue this career or that career?" Later on in life, the call
we *hear* might simply be about being and remaining faithful
(not necessarily an easy task) to our duties in our daily lives.
We might not even feel a great need to discern a particular
path to follow, as long as we are sure it's on the straight and
narrow path that leads to heaven.

Oftentimes, our lives unfold in ways we never imagined.
For instance, a married woman might yearn for many children but sadly find out after she's married that she is physically unable to conceive or carry a baby to full term. Another
married woman might dream of a perfect and happy life
but, because she marries a troubled man who abuses drugs
and alcohol, find her dreams shattered in discord and
divorce. Still another woman might not plan on a specific

career or vocation but is unpredictably delighted later on to discover her true calling through a series of unexpected experiences, events, and doors opening for her. Our lives seem to be shrouded in such mystery as we travel through our days unaware of the whole tapestry of our lives. We have but a glimpse of it now—a tiny glimpse.

When I was a little girl, with a sparkle in her eyes, my grandmother often told me, "Donna-Marie, if you become a nun, you'll go straight to heaven!" She so sweetly planted seeds of encouragement in my heart to seek a holy life. Her words intrigued me, and I often wondered if I would become a nun. My calling was revealed when I married and became a mother. Each day naturally unfolded in the tasks of loving service to others, totally meshed in the lives of the human beings God entrusted to my care. God's graces, which oftentimes seem profoundly hidden in the ordinary things, became more apparent to me as blessings abounded through the thick and thin of the vocation of motherhood— when life was going smoothly and also when life was arduous, as a single mother later on.

As a baptized Catholic woman, I can be certain that I *belong* to the family, the community, the Church, and the world! Whatever my circumstances and however my life is unfolding, I truly belong! Our Lord said, "Come, follow Me." I have a beautiful identity in the Lord and in the Church. And that exalted identity profoundly grounds me; it helps me to have peace of heart no matter what is happening in my life. As an act of faith, I answer God's call to my heart.

Blessed John Paul II reminds us, "Every vocation is a deep personal experience of the truth of these words: 'I am with you'" (Ex 3:12; homily, January 13, 1995). He is truly with us!

We'll look at that reality of our identities further throughout the book. In the next chapter, we'll explore what it means to be a *whole* woman. We'll look at the multiple dimensions in our personhood—our mind, heart, soul, and body.

A Moment to Reflect

Blessed John Paul II preached,

> The Lord tells the Prophet Jeremiah that his vocation was part of God's eternal plan even before he was born. . . . These words remind us that each person has a place in God's plan and that each of us should carefully listen to God's voice in prayer in order to discover the special calling we have received in Christ. (homily, September 2, 1990)

What a gift it is to be a Catholic woman! We enter the Church through Baptism as a baby or later in life and strive to work out our salvation through our lives each day, right in the nitty-gritty details in whatever walk of life we experience as a woman. And throughout it all, if we listen carefully to God's voice through prayer, we can be radiant examples to other women around us who might be struggling with their identities. We can pray for grace from God to be able to fulfill our own personal duties and become an incredible light to others.

My Mind to Know Him

1. Do you make a point of learning more about your faith so you can learn more about God and hopefully pass on your knowledge to those in your life?

2. Do you spend too much time on modern media and, because of this, not give enough time to learning your faith? If so, what are some ways you can cut back on social media, television, the Internet, and so on?

3. How can you schedule time to learn more about your Catholic faith and more time for solid spiritual reading?

My Heart to Love Him

1. Do you regularly tell God you love him? What are some tangible ways you can show him you love him?

2. Have you thought about your prayer life lately? Are there steps you can take to improve it?

3. Do you make time for God? Do you pause to listen to him? Can you tweak your schedule even a little to include God more fully in your life?

My Hands to Serve Him

1. Have you prayed about ways to serve God more concretely? Can you take time soon to think about it?

2. List the people in your life you feel our Lord would like you to serve in some way? Could there be someone you are missing?

3. How can you minister to someone very soon with Christ's love in a very simple way?

Seeking God

Dear Lord, open my heart to you entirely so I may fully experience all you are offering me and discover myself completely in you. Amen.

2. $\mathscr{B}$ECOMING A WHOLE WOMAN

> Love, which is of God, communicates itself
> to creatures: "God's love has been poured
> into our hearts through the Holy Spirit who
> has been given to us" (Rom 5:5).
>
> —*Mulieris Dignitatem* 29

Once, an elderly woman with whom I was talking on the phone said to me, "Just a minute, let me get my glasses so I can hear you better." This sounds funny, but it's quite possible that she really could hear better when she could see more clearly. We are complete beings made up of many components—a mind, a heart, a soul, and a body. In *Gaudium et Spes*, the *Pastoral Constitution on the Church in the Modern World* of Vatican II, we learn, "Man, though made of body and soul, is a unity" (*GS* 14). Our spirituality affects our whole being, not solely our hearts or our souls. If our bodies are not well, our souls can be affected too, especially if we don't have the right attitude about our illness or the challenges we are enduring. If our hearts are in the wrong place, well, naturally, our souls will be as well. If we're constantly daydreaming or wrapping our minds around unholy things, our minds will be the detriment of our souls. Everything is connected!

Pope Benedict has said, "Human spirituality invests the totality of the person, body and soul" (homily, January 7, 2007). Throughout this chapter we'll discuss the need to take care of our whole selves properly before we can appropriately follow the two great commandments to love God and also our neighbor. We'll also discover that we find wholeness within Christ.

And since we are women, sometimes caring for ourselves is no easy task. So many others depend on us, and our time is stretched. Yet, we need to be as well as we can be in our wholeness in order to function proficiently and to reach out ably to others.

Our Hearts

Let's start with our hearts—it's quite obvious that women have huge hearts! Just take a look around and you'll see that countless women are caring for others in multiple ways. God made us that way—to receive love and give love. In *Mulieris Dignitatem, On the Dignity and Vocation of Women,* Blessed John Paul II said, "A woman's dignity is closely connected with the love which she receives by very reason of her femininity; it is likewise connected with the love which she gives in return. . . . Woman can only find herself by giving love to others" (*MD* 30).

Each and every woman is a mother to others, whether biological, adoptive, or spiritual. It is innate. Women are given motherly hearts by God specifically to care for others—to nurture relationships, encourage, uplift, ease pain, bring peace, and "soothe the savage beast"—to mother them!

We learn through our Church, "The moral and spiritual strength of a woman is joined to her awareness that *God entrusts the human being to her in a special way*. Of course, God entrusts every human being to each and every other human being. But this entrusting concerns women in a special way—precisely by reason of her femininity—and this in a particular way determines their vocation" (*MD* 30).

The key word here is *awareness*. Awareness is required on our part regarding God's amazing gift of the human being to us so that we can fully comprehend our vocation as a feminine woman. If I am caught up in the values (or lack thereof) of the culture, the mass media, excessive shopping, idiotic reality television, and spending endless time on the Internet, I might totally miss God speaking to me regarding his entrusting of others to me—I won't be aware. How could I possibly be? It's not even just the lack of time I'll have left to hear God and converse with him. It's also that the other things (which are not holy) will pollute my heart and make it much more difficult for me to find my way out of the muck, especially if I am becoming numb to its ill effects or even enjoying it. And if God is counting on us women to make a difference in our world and to draw others to him, by our lives of Christian love, well, we will have failed him. We will have fallen for the "apple" as did Eve.

We must also pray to find a proper balance regarding the activities we engage in and the community service and ministry work we do. As I said earlier, women's hearts are huge, and we want to help others in many ways, but we must not neglect the very ones our Lord has put in our midst for us to care for—the ones he has entrusted to us. Blessed Mother Teresa was forever preaching that "love begins at home." Let's be sure we have our priorities straight. A good gauge is to ponder all of the needs of those you care for in some way. Are the needs fulfilled? Do you have extra time, energy, and inclination to broaden your reach of ministry and love? Our Lord will guide you if you ask him in prayer. Granted, we won't always feel the energy! At times, we will have to push through our weariness to do God's holy will.

In *The Little Prince*, Antoine de Saint-Exupéry said, "It is only with the heart that one can see rightly. What is essential is invisible to the eye." How can we nurture and care for our own hearts so that we can "see rightly"? We do so with prayer (which we'll get into more in chapter 4), with pondering God's never-ending love for us, by allowing others to love us.

The sacraments illustrate God's immense love for us. In receiving Holy Communion, we receive Jesus who gives us strength for our daily journey. Confession frees us from sin and gives us grace. Meditating on the gospels and other good spiritual reading, such as the lives of the saints, can help us more fully understand God's love and will nurture and inspire our hearts to come nearer to him.

One time Jesus was invited by a Pharisee to his home for dinner. After Jesus sat down to dine, a city woman came to the house carrying an alabaster jar of ointment. The woman was moved to tears at Jesus' feet, covering his feet with her tears and her kisses and wiping them with her locks of hair. She proceeded to anoint Jesus' sacred feet with the balm, showing her great love for him while no doubt feeling sorry for her sins. The Pharisee complained bitterly because he knew the woman was a sinner. Maybe he was even a bit jealous of the woman. Jesus pointed out that the Pharisee who had invited him had not greeted him with a kiss, nor had he washed his feet of the dust from his travels or anointed his head. The woman, on the other hand, had not stopped kissing Jesus since he arrived. Jesus then said, "Therefore, I tell you, her sins, which were many, have been forgiven; hence she has shown great love. But the one to whom little is forgiven, loves little. Then he said to her, 'Your sins are forgiven'" (Lk 7:36–50).

Jesus was known to transcend the culture of his own time and show women great understanding, tenderness, and love. In *Mulieris Dignitatem*, Blessed John Paul II said, "In all of Jesus' teaching, as well as in his behavior, one can find nothing which reflects the discrimination against women prevalent in his day. On the contrary, his words and works always express the respect and honor due to women" (*MD* 13). This same Jesus is with us today in the Eucharist, in tabernacles around the world, and is living within us.

God's eminent love for women heartens us. It encourages us to go to meet him with our sins, to kiss his feet and wash them with our repentant tears. He will forgive us and heal our hearts completely. Let's not fear approaching him in our prayers and through the sacraments, especially Confession. If you are hesitant for any reason, think about Blessed John Paul II 's words, "Be not afraid!"

OUR MINDS

The mind is a complicated thing. Most definitions of the mind describe it as constituted by conscious experience and intelligent thought. Perception, reason, memory, imagination, emotion, attention, and a capacity for communication are usually listed among the common attributes of mind. And although psychologists debate about all of the functions and emotions that occupy the conscious and the unconscious mind, a rich set of unconscious processes are also included in many modern characterizations of the mind. Some psychologists say that the emotions of joy, fear, love, and hate are subjective in nature and should be viewed as different from the mind.

Brain science is a growing field today. It includes the study of the two hemispheres of the brain, the nervous system and immune system's relationship with the brain, how our bodies and minds work together, how the mind reasons, where emotions come from, and on and on. While I am not an authority on the human mind, I am attempting to discuss the mind as an integral component of our wholeness.

From a Christian perspective, the mind should be stimulated and nourished regularly with solid faith-oriented material—not garbage. I say this because the mind is like a sponge that constantly absorbs and retains information. When you put garbage in your mind—via bad movies, music, television, gossip, pornography, and images and things that are not holy—it will remain there forever to haunt you, popping up at the most inopportune times.

What's worse, the evil one (yes, it's true, he exists!) will exploit the "garbage" you've allowed in your mind to his advantage and attempt to trip you up, tempt you, distract you, and basically use it to drive you crazy.

We can inadvertently overstimulate our minds with overuse of the Internet, social media, television, video games, and the like. It's best to avoid too much stimulation of the mind before bedtime to allow your brain to settle and your body to ease into sleep. Spiritual reading before bedtime, along with prayer, is very soothing to the mind. Let's also consider "unplugging" completely, at least once in a while, from technology. I find Sundays a great day to back away from social media and the Internet if possible. When we do, we have more time for observing the Sabbath in the ways that we should.

I really believe that too many of us are caught up in social media to an unhealthy degree. Social media can be a wonderful area in which to connect with like-minded faithful people. I use Facebook, Twitter, my website, and blogs to evangelize. Even so, I need to be sure I don't let social media take over my life. I can't be using it all the time.

We all need to ask ourselves how much time this media takes away from the real life conversations and encounters that our good Lord would want us engaging in. I can almost see it now: we're at someone's funeral, and the casket is surrounded by laptops, notebooks, and smart phones instead of people! Perhaps we should ask ourselves, are we too busy with our virtual relationships to attend to the real people in our lives?

Since we are focusing on the mind, I'd like to mention that there is such a thing as "custody of the senses," an expression not often used these days. Father John A. Hardon explains:

> In Christian asceticism, there is the practice of controlling the use of the senses, especially the eyes, in order to foster union with God and preserve oneself in virtue. It is founded on the premise that "nothing is in the mind that was not first in the senses." Sense experience inevitably produces thoughts in the mind; thoughts become desires; and desires lead to actions. Morally good actions, therefore, ultimately depend on a judicious guard of sensations.[1]

Let's be cognizant that what we allow into our minds will stay there and can either enlighten and nurture us or corrupt us if we are lackadaisical or simply allow it to. We need to make a conscious decision not to engage in unholy media and activities.

Certainly, we are not completely in control of the stuff that gets into our minds since many stimuli and images surround us on any given day and even every moment. But we can turn our eyes from unholy things as best we can and whisper up a Hail Mary asking our Blessed Mother to protect us from its ill effects. St. Thomas Aquinas said, "Man's most perfect thoughts are those which are about God. Turn your thoughts often to God."

OUR SOULS

We can't do a CAT scan or an MRI of the soul. Yet, we believe it exists somewhere in us and is a part of us. It truly is at the core of our being. The Church teaches that we are all gifted with an immortal soul that was immediately created by God at the moment of our conception. Our soul never perishes, and at the moment we die, our soul is separated from our body until they are reunited at the final resurrection.

The *Catechism* tells us that "it is because of its spiritual soul that the body made of matter becomes a living, human body; spirit and matter" (CCC 365). Our souls animate us with life! It is our grave responsibility to care for our souls. As I spoke earlier about our minds and the need to be watchful and vigilant regarding what we allow them to ponder, so too we need to care tenderly for our souls.

Our souls will become stagnant without proper nourishment. The all-time best food for our souls is prayer. Feed your soul first and foremost with prayer. Seek God in prayer in your walk of life as a Catholic woman. Make room for him in your life, and ask him to bring you ever closer to him. St. Francis de Sales said, "Half an hour's meditation is essential except when you are very busy. Then a full hour is needed." No doubt he meant that, if we are too busy to meditate and pray, we are lost. We need to make sure we pray and meditate more when we're stressed and extra busy—we need it. Before you throw in the towel, thinking that you just don't have the time, consider that your prayer can be naturally woven in with your activities. God is always with you, waiting for you to strike up a conversation. No formalities are necessary—speak up! (We will explore the many forms of prayer in chapter 4.)

Father Hardon preached, "The soul is meant to be alive twice over. As a spiritual reality, our soul will never cease to exist. But if our soul is not animated by the grace we received at Baptism, we shall die the double death of both body and soul."[2] Grace is food for our souls. If we are in sin, our soul is dying.

The care of our souls is serious business. St. Augustine preached, "Take care of your body as if you were going to live forever; take care of your soul as if you were going to die tomorrow." This sober thought we should take to heart. We need to live each day as if it were our last and really and truly prepare our souls.

Father Hardon counseled that we should only keep company with people who are obviously in the state of grace because they can indeed aid us on our spiritual journeys. Many times at retreats and to me personally he warned that hanging out with people who aren't so concerned about the state of their souls might very well be to our detriment. We should of course minister to the sinner if we are called to, but we should not take on the bad habits of sinners and allow their influence to take over our own minds and souls. If our friends are comprised of mostly non-Christians and nonbelievers, we can expect that their influence will not be nurturing our souls.

We can also feed our souls with spiritual reading. But we need to be sure that the material we study is in line with authentic Church teaching. Father Hardon said,

> Make absolutely sure that in studying the faith you read authors who support the faith, and consult people who themselves are staunchly Catholic, and listen to speakers and attend conferences and discuss with those who will

fortify what you believe. Let their faith nourish yours
and your faith, nourish theirs. Never has it been more
necessary to choose your close friends and companions.[3]

St. John Bosco shared his beliefs and cautions on spiritual readings: "Never read books you are not sure about . . .
even supposing these bad books are very well written from
a literary point of view. Let me ask you this: would you
drink something you knew had been poisoned just because
it was offered to you in a golden cup?"[4] This brings to mind
the numerous books out there that are not in line with the
Church's teaching and the others that are a total attack on
Church tradition. We must be wise and selective. If you're
not sure, check it out with someone who is sure.

Many who want to advance in holiness pursue spiritual
direction. It's wise to seek out a holy priest, religious, or
someone you know who is knowledgeable with matters of
the spiritual life and faithful to the magisterium (or teaching authority of the Church), and, of course, someone who
is willing to meet with you on a regular basis to discuss
spiritual matters and growth.

St. John of the Cross recommended that the person desiring to advance in holiness should "take care into whose
hands he entrusts himself, for as the master is, so will the
disciple be, and as the father is so will be the son." He
warned that the spiritual director should be experienced in
the spiritual life and that, if he isn't, "he will be incapable
of leading into it the souls whom God is calling to it, and
he will not even understand them." Choose your spiritual
director wisely.

OUR BODIES

Our bodies house us—house our spirits. Our bodies are tem-
ples of the Holy Spirit. Our bodies have been made in God's

own image. We are told by the Church, "The human body shares in the dignity of the 'image of God': it is a human body precisely because it is animated by a spiritual soul, and it is the whole human person that is intended to become, in the body of Christ, a temple of the Spirit" (CCC 364).

When I feel well and am healthy I am better able to do the things I should do and better able to care for others who are entrusted to my care. I'm reminded of a story my friend Father Peter Towsley shared with me. He told me that many years ago he brought a group of seminarians to the convent where Mother Teresa was visiting. The young men were going to have a meal there and Mother Teresa would pay them a visit. She entered the dining room when everyone was seated and approached the table. She noticed that one man's plate didn't have much food on it. So, in a kind of dramatic motion, she quickly lifted a huge serving tray and scraped a lot of the food onto the young seminarian's plate. She leaned in and quietly said, "You can't take care of others very well if you'll be worrying about your hungry belly." I'm sure she got the point across to that seminarian and the whole group of them! Her words can help us, too.

Another friend, Father Bill Smith, was really like a second father to me. When he was about eighty years old, he knew I was tremendously busy every day with family and work. He would often recommend that I take a little daily siesta after lunch: "Wouldn't you like to lie down, Donna? Just take a little nap after lunch like I do." "Of course I would like to, Father Bill, but I have a lot to do!" Well, even though I don't think I'll be taking an afternoon nap any time soon, his wisdom is something we can all take to heart. We need to give our bodies the rest they need. I try to do that at night by getting to bed at a reasonable hour. It doesn't always work out that way, but I do try because I know that when I lack the proper amount of sleep, I feel the repercussions the next day. I can't perform at my best. And God is counting on me to do my best.

I really like what St. Thomas Aquinas said: "Sorrow can be alleviated by good sleep, a bath, and a glass of wine."Even the saints spoke about caring for our bodies to remedy our sorrows or other maladies. St. Thomas also said, "It is requisite for the relaxation of the mind that we make use, from time to time, of playful deeds and jokes." In other words, we can't be all about only work and no play! We can't take ourselves so seriously that we don't have occasion to laugh. Laughter, after all, is a very good medicine for the heart, soul, mind, and body.

St. Josemaria Escrivá spoke about the need for rest and refreshment:

> I have always seen rest as time set aside from daily tasks, never as days of idleness.
>
> Rest means recuperation: to gain strength, form ideals and make plans. In other words it means a change of occupation, so that you can come back later with a new impetus to your daily job.[5]

St. Francis de Sales has said, "From time to time one must recreate and relax in mind and body. . . . It is actually a defect to be so strict, austere and unsociable that one permits neither himself nor others any recreation time" (*Introduction to the Devout Life*).

I often have to walk away from the computer when deep into a writing project to seek a change of scenery, to get a breath of fresh air, move around, and say a prayer. Inevitably, when away from the task at hand, even momentarily, the inspiration comes. The monks of St. Benedict and many other monastic orders have a specific time slot for rest and recreation scheduled into their busy days. They make sure to nurture the whole person.

We've heard it said, "Listen to your body." Yet, sometimes that is so tough for a woman to do, especially if she's feeling sad or preoccupied with so much stuff or if she's burning the candle at both ends. When we can't exactly *hear* our body very well a domino effect occurs. It can be a long spiral down when we are too preoccupied to realize that our bodies are screaming for proper nutrition and rest.

That's where balance comes in. We must strive to become a balanced person. Sure, at times we are all fired up and running around like a maniac trying to get something accomplished, but hopefully these times are few and far between. On a regular basis we want to be on an even keel and cognizant of our body's needs for proper health and nutrition and try, when possible, to proceed at an even pace. So, even when we are crazy busy, we will have previously planned the nutrition and rest we require.

An integral part of our wellness of body is to be sure that we are getting exercise appropriate for our age and circumstances. We also need to eat well. I am a firm believer in nourishing our bodies with healthy foods, hopefully organic when possible. I grow a huge organic garden each year at my home in the foothills of Connecticut that includes lots of garlic, which I consider to be a natural antibiotic and a great immune booster. I use garlic in most of the meals I cook. I'm always slipping it in! If I'm coming down with an illness, I'll be sure to eat some raw garlic (yes, that's right, raw!) each day along with extra vitamin C and B vitamins that get used up by our bodies quickly when we are under stress or are sick. I also like to use healthy whole grains in my cooking and to eat lots of fresh fruits and vegetables, and take vitamin and mineral supplements.

When I can, I make my own breads and yogurt, granola, muffins, and healthy cookies. I often make big pots of healthy soup and freeze a portion for later on as well as

give some away to a shut-in or someone I know who is sick
and could use some healthy nourishment. There's nothing
like a hot bowl of nutritious soup—made with love—for the
body, heart, and soul! Also, be sure to take the medications
prescribed for you in a timely manner and be aware of any
ill effects that you should report to your doctor.

We couldn't possibly end a chapter on being a whole
woman without expressing that it is in Christ that we discover our wholeness and where we will find a divine rest. St.
Augustine has said, "Thou hast made us for thyself, O Lord,
and our hearts are restless until they find their rest in thee."
He reminds us that we won't acquire rest in the things of this
world, but only in our Lord. The rest he speaks of is peace
of heart and soul. No matter how busy we are or whatever
our circumstances, when we come to really know and love
our Lord, we will find a glorious *rest* in him.

A MOMENT TO REFLECT

Jesus offers us great joy! He lets us in on the secret to great
joy and that is to keep his commandments. When someone
asked Jesus, "Teacher, which commandment in the law is
the greatest?" Jesus replied,

> You shall love the Lord your God with all your heart,
> and with your soul, and with all your mind. This is the
> greatest and the first commandment. And a second is
> like it: You shall love your neighbor as yourself. On these
> two commandments hang all the law and the prophets.
> (Mt 22:36–41)

Father Hardon would often say, "We must love God with
our whole mind, our whole heart, our whole soul, and our
strength until the day we die." He would repeat it again to
be sure he was heard clearly and that we understood fully.

At the end of his life when he was suffering terribly with cancer throughout his body, he offered his intense affliction to God for the needs of Holy Mother Church. I learned much from my friend who was an exemplary example of a soul animated with an exceptional love for God and one who anticipated his eternal reward. In fact, his catch phrase was "There's work to be done!" It was more than a saying. Father Hardon would throw his arms up in a particular way each time he said it, and his eyes would light right up. He was always cognizant of our responsibilities to further the kingdom of God and tirelessly work toward it. If anyone entered heaven exhausted, it was Father Hardon!

In *Abandonment to Divine Providence*, Father Jean-Pierre de Caussade said, "Everything has a supernatural quality, something divine about it that can lead us onward to holiness. Everything is part of that completeness which is Jesus Christ." Let's try to view everything in our lives in that light.

As we discover our wholeness in Christ, let's call to mind that "woman can only find herself by giving love to others" (*MD* 30); let's strive our very best to love God with all our hearts, souls, and minds so that we are fully able to love our neighbor as ourselves. Let's also bear in mind that we have the responsibility to care for our bodies, hearts, minds, and souls the best we can. When we are well in our wholeness we are able to love God and our neighbor.

My Mind to Know Him

1. How might you become more aware of your own God-given dignity as a woman?

2. What steps can you take to learn more about your dig-
    nity as a Catholic woman? Can you list three?

3. What steps can you take to schedule appropriate times
    for rest into your schedule? Can you take some time
    to ponder ways to eat healthier as well? Can you take
    steps to "unplug" from too much technology to give
    your brain a rest?

My Heart to Love Him

1. Do you take the time to ponder God's never-ending love
    for you—for exclusively you?

2. Do you love God through your conversations with him
    and your prayers to him?

3. What is a tangible way to show God your love that you
    can put into practice this week?

My Hands to Serve Him

1. List three ways you can endeavor to help other women
    discover or recognize their own God-given dignity, espe-
    cially the women you feel are suffering because they are
    not aware of their dignity in God's eyes.

2. Do you try your best to take the time to encourage and
    help others in your midst—family, neighbors, and peo-
    ple you see when you are out and about?

3. Do you try to do your everyday tasks lovingly and faith-
    fully in your role as a Catholic woman?

Seeking God

Dear Lord Jesus, help me to discover the holy balance you want me to achieve in living my life as a whole woman. Amen.

PART TWO

CHRIST IS MY STRENGTH

For in him we live and move and have our being.

—Acts 17:28

3. $\mathscr{A}$LWAYS AT MY SIDE

How lovely is your dwelling place, O Lord
of hosts!

—Psalm 84:1

Women perpetually have their hands and hearts in any number of projects, activities, and chores. We are endlessly working to teach, nurture, create change, ease pain, and bring comfort and good cheer to family members and beyond—as well as a zillion other things! And because we are so involved and engaged, we can sometimes lose sight of God's divine presence in our lives because of our busyness. Yet, truth be told, God is always by our sides. Unfortunately, though, we might be too busy to recognize him.

Many women with whom I have spoken over the years have told me how enormously stretched they usually feel on any given day. Their lives are filled to the brim with activity and concerns. Through taking care of their families and households, working outside the home, and volunteering, they say they sometimes feel they are racing from one activity to the next, all the while burdened with a constant worry about having enough hours in the day to complete their tasks. I can totally relate!

All this running around and worrying can cause women to lose touch with God in their lives, and possibly bring ill health, too. Yet, God is always there. Knowing and believing that he is there can be a great comfort to a woman's heart. And that is actually the real reason I am writing this book—to bring that comfort to a woman's heart!

Perhaps we should begin by remembering that God is actually seeking us out even if we are not actively seeking him. We are so utterly blessed to have a God that loves us that much! Some women, although active, have not lost sight of the fact that our Lord is right by their sides. However, they wonder when exactly they can pencil him in for a chat because they are forever racing against the clock.

"The Lord Is Near"

We read in the Psalms, "The Lord is near to all who call on him" (Ps 145:18). It's so imperative for us to schedule times to pray throughout our busy days and to try to stick to those times so we can "call on him." Prayer is a prerequisite for keeping our sanity intact, too!

Simply because we are women, we are often interrupted (especially we mothers) by people who need our assistance in some form or another. I'm sure this is not news to you. We might wish to continue our scheduled conversation with the Lord, but we, in a sense, excuse ourselves from that particular prayer for a time to serve him within the person who is asking for our help at that moment—the crying child, the upset teenager, the visiting neighbor, the needy coworker, our perplexed spouse, and so on.

A wonderful example of this form of prayer (yes, it is prayer!) was practiced by Blessed Teresa of Calcutta who spent about fifty years serving Jesus in others, specifically in whom she called "the poorest of the poor." For the necessary

strength to do her work among the poor, lonely, and devastated in Calcutta and all around the world, Mother Teresa
first fueled herself with deep prayer through the holy sacrifice of the Mass, the sacraments, the Rosary, and Eucharistic Adoration. She was very much aware through the gift
of faith that God was indeed with her, even if by outward
appearances he didn't always seem to be. With that arsenal
of prayer power under her belt, she was then able to meet
each need as it was presented in her work. This doesn't
mean it was effortless—not at all. Most times it was arduous,
and she needed to push herself physically and spiritually
to do the work.

Blessed Teresa of Calcutta truly believed she was ministering to Jesus Christ within each and every person she
served, from the lowliest of the poverty-stricken and dying
persons she saved from the gutters to the popes she con-
sulted with and Princess Diana with whom she spent some
time. She even had time for me, a suburban housewife! Each
person became Jesus to her.

She could do this because she wholeheartedly lived and
breathed the words of Jesus, who said, "Truly I tell you, just
as you did it to one of the least of these who are members
of my family, you did it to me" (Mt 25:40). Mother Teresa's
whole life revolved around that.

Each one of us women can live that same Gospel message and seek to discover Jesus within each person we come
in contact with, too. We will look at this concept more thoroughly in other areas of this book.

GETTING OUR DAY STARTED

I always start my day with a morning offering so that I can
offer everything in advance to God when I first open my
eyes to a new day. Before I dive into a usually thoroughly

jam-packed schedule, I get on my knees and I offer our Lord my prayers, works, joys, and sufferings of that day right by the side of my bed. I ask him to use it all for his glory, to sanctify everything, and to unite it all to his sufferings on the Cross and the holy sacrifice of the Mass, and I pray for souls in need of help, especially the suffering souls in purgatory and those in danger of dying. Of course, I always add my requests for help for all my family members and friends.

You can pray a formal morning offering prayer. There are many variations of this form of prayer. I like to use the traditional morning offering of the Apostleship of Prayer that was recommended to me by Cardinal Raymond Leo Burke:

> O Jesus, through the Immaculate Heart of Mary, I offer you my prayers, works, joys and sufferings of this day in union with the Holy Sacrifice of the Mass throughout the world. I offer them for all the intentions of Your Sacred heart: the salvation of souls, reparation for sins, the reunion of all Christians. I offer them for the intentions of Your Bishops and all Apostles of Prayer and in particular for those recommended by our Holy Father this month. Amen.

Or you can simply pray in your own heartfelt words to offer in advance the merits of your day. I do a combination of the two. The great thing about a morning offering is that you are surrendering everything over to God as you start your day. In this way, you are giving him complete control—handing him the reins. By doing so, you in essence are freeing yourself of worrying about how things will unfold throughout the day. All of the challenges, craziness, joys, and everything that presents itself will be enveloped in a trusting prayer to God. He will be with you and help you in every detail of your day. It's a simple prayer requiring very little time and effort, but when sincerely and lovingly presented to God, it will guarantee that your life that day is shrouded in his infinite grace and love—no matter what happens!

One time I was discussing the profound beauty in the morning offering with my friend Father Peter Towsley. I told him, "I firmly believe the morning offering prayer is one of the most important prayers ever. In it, we offer all of our prayers, works, joys, and sufferings of the day in advance and ask our Lord to unite them to him and the holy sacrifice of the Mass, and he will transform them with his love and grace." I added, "God can bring so much good out of everything—no matter what happens that day—we can be comforted knowing he is always in control." I share this story here to illustrate how God uses us to reach others when we surrender our lives to him in prayer and trust him to do the work through us.

That very night my husband, Dave, experienced excruciating pains in his abdomen and chest and severe vomiting that necessitated a hurried trip to the emergency room. It was the second time something like this had happened in the past week, and this time we knew it must not be a simple stomach bug; we needed emergency help.

Within minutes after arriving at the hospital, the emergency staff had Dave hooked up to just about every machine and started an IV. Blood samples were drawn and soon after revealed a very serious infection brewing somewhere in his body. A subsequent CAT scan detected Dave's gallbladder as the location of the infection. It had to come out immediately, and there was grave danger of the infection getting even more out of control.

Just like that! Within such a short period of time our lives seemed to turn totally upside down. We were at the mercy of God. Well, we are always at his mercy, but sometimes that reality seems more in our face. We prayed together, and I sent prayer request messages out to family and friends. I knew that, despite the apparent uncertainty we faced, I could be certain in my heart that God was in charge—that he would take care of us even better than we could have hoped for. I had given everything to him in my morning offering and asked for his holy will to be done in my life. He would come through in his divine way—whatever that was.

Dave was wheeled into surgery at 3:00 p.m., the Hour of Great Mercy. God was reminding me of his presence in my husband's and my life and his unsurpassed perfect timing. It also happened to be the Feast of St. Padre Pio, and the saint's famous teaching, "Pray, hope, and don't worry!" brought me further comfort and great hope. I counted on God's presence and his promises.

The operation went very well. Afterward the surgeon told me about the infected gallbladder he removed and details of the surgery. "It was horrible!" he said. "Five more minutes and I would have cut him wide open!" I told him I believed that it was God's grace and God's perfect timing that gave us that wonderful outcome.

He said, "You're not kidding; it was the grace of God!"

It was music to my ears to hear the surgeon acknowledge that God indeed had his divine hand in this. Because of God's perfect timing, Dave was able to have laparoscopic surgery done and thus a much easier recovery.

In addition to Dave's incredible surgery in God's perfect timing and his wonderful recovery, many beautiful transformations took place, and we experienced many special encounters with the hospital staff in which I openly shared my faith. God's graces were flowing on that third floor!

During Dave's surgery, I met JoAn, the wife of a man who had a gallbladder removal prior to my husband's surgery. She and I chatted in the quiet surgical waiting room and found a great deal of comfort in one another's presence. We also prayed together for our husbands, and I felt inspired to give this woman two blessed Miraculous Medals while we were waiting for our husbands to go through their surgeries and recoveries. I carry blessed medals with me in my purse (in the spirit of Mother Teresa who gave them to those she met) because I often give them out, sometimes in the most unusual places (like a gelato counter in Rome).

As we sat together waiting, JoAn started to tell me a little about her faith journey and the fact that she and her husband John were searching for a church in which to worship. Right then, I whispered up prayers for JoAn and John and hoped that God would use me to bring them into the Church (especially since they were searching!). I shared with her that I was a Catholic author and pulled out a copy of my newest book *Mother Teresa and Me: Ten Years of Friendship* to show her. Naturally, that lent fodder to our conversation. I ended up giving that copy of the book to Dave's surgeon.

The next day, JoAn and I found one another, and I gave her a copy of my Mother Teresa book. Each day at the hospital, we embraced, conversed, and prayed for one another's husbands. My husband had to get rid of a terrible infection, and JoAn's husband had to get over some critical health hurdles and regain his strength.

Since JoAn was afforded time alone at home while her husband John was in the hospital, she devoured the book I gave her. She told me that my book brought her tremendous comfort, and because of the blessings she felt coming through me to her, she had decided along with her husband to start going to church again!

Later on, after our husbands were discharged, JoAn told me by e-mail that she and her husband were wearing the Miraculous Medals. John, who had suffered terribly with nightmares every night since his open-heart surgery many years prior, had not had one nightmare since wearing his medal.

God brings amazing blessings from our sufferings when offered to him in love, which we can do every morning and throughout each day. I had no doubt that God was working powerfully on this couples' hearts at the hospital and afterward. St. Paul tells us, "We know that all things work together for good for those who love God" (Rom 8:28).

And to think, before all of this transpired, Dave and I were dreaming about and even pondering a way to pull off a mini-getaway trip. I think God really has a great sense of humor. We were yearning for a respite—just a little time away—even a weekend, to relax since we both had been putting in endless hours with our work to meet deadlines. Instead of a restful beach getaway, God gave us special time to be together in the hospital ER and a stay at the hospital!

I am reminded of words from Paul's Letter to the Philippians:

> Rejoice in the Lord always; again I will say, Rejoice. Let your gentleness be known to everyone. The Lord is near. Do not worry about anything, but in everything by prayer and supplication with thanksgiving let your requests be made known to God. And the peace of God, which surpasses all understanding, will guard your hearts and your minds in Christ Jesus. (Phil 4:4–8)

"BE STILL, AND KNOW THAT I AM GOD"

One of my favorite reminders of God present in my life and the fact that he wants me to rest in him is found in the words "Be still, and know that I am God!" (Ps 46:10), which are displayed on a little plaque on my desk. These words prompt me to pause and remember that God is with me and he wants me to know that no matter what is happening around me, even as I am up to my elbows in a project, housekeeping, or struggling through a challenging situation, I can interiorly pause to "be still" in the Lord—even if just to say, *I am here Lord. Thank you for being here with me. Bless me please and help me to do this task well, drawing others to you by the love my soul bears to you.*

Sometimes, just an acknowledgment of God present to us through a simple heartfelt aspiration voiced interiorly can result in an amazing transformation for ourselves and others around us.

MEETING JESUS AT THE WELL OF PRAYER

I'm sure you are very familiar with the wonderful account of Jesus meeting the Samaritan woman at Jacob's well (Jn 4:7–27). Jesus' disciples had gone into the town to buy food, and Jesus, being tired from his journey, sat down by the well. A Samaritan woman came to the well to draw water around noon. Jesus said to her, "Give me a drink." The woman was confused initially because men (especially Jews) did not speak to Samaritans at all, much less to a woman!

Rather than get into a long explanation at that point as to why he was speaking to her, Jesus continued, "If you knew the gift of God, and who it is that is saying to you, 'Give me a drink,' you would have asked him, and he would have given you living water."

The woman wanted to know how she could get some of this extraordinary living water of which this intriguing man was speaking. The conversation went on for a while, and Jesus explained that it is not the water from the well that will quench our true thirst but rather the living water. He said, "The water that I will give will become in them a spring of water gushing up to eternal life."

Through Jesus' questioning about her sinful life, the Samaritan woman became enlightened that this mysterious man at the well was indeed the Messiah. Jesus said, "I am he, the one who is speaking to you." The sinful woman, who we might venture to say was there at noon (the hottest part of the day) to avoid bumping into anyone because she was ashamed, was amazed and transformed so much so that she left her water jar at the well and hurried back to her village to tell her people what had transpired. They then traveled back to the well to find Jesus.

Pope John Paul II spoke about the marvelous exchange between Jesus and the woman: "The conversation leading up to this realization is one of the most beautiful in the Gospel" (*MD* 13).

Jesus calls every woman to the well of *living water*. He longs for a conversation with us. Just as Jesus sought the Samaritan woman, so also he wants to meet with us. Just as the Samaritan woman freely spoke to Jesus, so we can, too. Just as Jesus told the woman about her sinful past, so also he wants to speak to us about ours and offer us forgiveness and mercy. He imparts the living water to us, continuously nourishing us and satiating our deepest longings for the Truth. We'll discover the Truth in Jesus Christ and not in our crazy world. Let's visit the well of prayer often to fill ourselves with Jesus' transforming love.

Praying with the Church

That marvelous sacrament of Baptism unites each and every one of us to God. Pope Benedict XVI explained, "Baptism will remain throughout life a gift of God, who has set his seal on our souls. But it will then be our cooperation, the availability of our freedom to say that 'yes' which makes divine action effective" (homily, January 7, 2007).

The *Catechism* explains, "Thus, the life of prayer is the habit of being in the presence of the thrice-holy God and in communion with him. This communion of life is always possible because, through Baptism, we have already been united with Christ. Prayer is *Christian* insofar as it is communion with Christ and extends throughout the Church, which is his Body. Its dimensions are those of Christ's love" (*CCC* 2565).

Each one of us can have a very personal and loving relationship with our Creator. We can say "yes" to him each day. The "yes" can be profound as well as simply and lovingly going about our duties and thanking God for our lives. As well, Catholic women are also united with God while in communion with the whole Church—the Body of Christ. Being a part of the Church helps us to come closer to God, through the liturgy and the sacraments. We are deeply nourished through the Body of Christ.

We enter the mystery of prayer through the gift of faith. Jesus asks us to cooperate with the divine plan and has taught us that "whatever you ask for in prayer, believe that you have received it, and it will be yours" (Mk 11:24). These are such powerful words to ponder in our hearts. We really should pray each day for an increase in the virtue of faith so that we can enter into prayer sincerely and lovingly and truly believe. Jesus has always responded to prayers from people of faith.

Many examples of Jesus' response to prayer are expressed in the scriptures: the leper (Mt 8:1–4), Jairus (Mk 5:41), the Canaanite woman (Mt 15:28), the good thief (Lk 23:43), the bearers of the paralytic (Mk 2:1–12), the woman with the hemorrhage who reaches out to touch Jesus' cloak (Mk 5:27–34), the tears and the ointment of the sinful woman (Lk 7:39–50), and the blind man who cried out, "Jesus, Son of David, have mercy on me!"(Mk 10:47–52)

We have a phenomenal helper in our prayer lives, for the Holy Spirit guides us in prayer. We know that, on the day of Pentecost, the Holy Spirit was poured out on all of the disciples who were gathered together in the upper room with the Blessed Mother—all praying for the Holy Spirit to come to them (Acts 2:1). The disciples united together in prayer, frightened and devastated after witnessing the cruel torment and subsequent Crucifixion of their Messiah, yet holding fast to the hope of the Holy Spirit that Jesus promised to send them. That same Holy Spirit who appeared on the day of Pentecost as wind and tongues of fire also inspires us Catholic women and moves our hearts to pray. Let's not forget to ask the Holy Spirit to guide us.

Throughout the Church's history, the Church's prayer was "founded on apostolic faith; authenticated by charity; nourished by the Eucharist" (*CCC* 2624). Scripture reveals to us that, in the first community of Jerusalem, believers "devoted themselves to the apostles' teaching and fellowship, to the breaking of bread and the prayers" (Acts 2:42).

We too, as Catholic women, devote ourselves to the teachings of the Church and have the privilege of sharing in the Eucharist together. We are joined in fellowship with one another through our rich Catholic faith. We are never alone even though we might feel isolated, whether we are mothering at home or caring for an elderly person, our prayers united with the prayers of the Church make us one.

Catholics can be very different in appearance and in the customs they practice in their native lands. Yet, the same fundamental faith is practiced by a staggering variety of peoples, separated by history, culture, and geography, but transcending these differences to become one in identity.

Perhaps this communion of Catholics of every race all contributing in their own way with their own gifts is best

explained in the *Dogmatic Constitution on the Church*, one of
the most important document of the Second Vatican Council:

> In virtue of this catholicity, each individual part brings
> its gifts to the other parts and to the entire Church, and
> thus the whole and individual parts are reinforced by
> communicating with each other, working together to
> attain fulfillment in unity. (*LG* 13)

We can also find similar sentiments in the New Testament, specifically in 1 Corinthians 12:12–27 and Romans
12:5.

Jesus comes to each one of us and expects us to spread
his love and joy to others. Blessed Teresa of Calcutta has
said, "Jesus is pleased to come to us as the truth to be told
and the life to be lived, as the light to be lighted and the
love to be loved, as the joy to be given and the peace to be
spread."

A MOMENT TO REFLECT

It is quite amazing that God remains by our sides even as
we are far from perfect in our lives. Such a loving God has
created us in his image and likeness and wants us to live
up to our high dignity and calling. He gives us countless
opportunities, even in the course of one day, to turn to him
in prayer for our needs and our lives.

Incredibly, God continues to seek us as we are "drawing
water" throughout the midst of our demanding days. No
matter how busy or distracted we might be, God is forever
seeking us out to converse with us, to love us!

He reminds us, "I will be with you" (Ex 3:12).

My Mind to Know Him

1. How can you put the knowledge you have of God's amazing presence in your life to better use? Do you pause to recognize it? Do you teach others about it? Do you share your faith in your family and beyond?

2. What can you do to learn more about God and the Church? Can you list three ideas?

3. Will you strive to learn more about the Church by reading the *Catechism*, perhaps some Church documents, or possibly gather together with others to study the faith?

My Heart to Love Him

1. What steps will you take to show God your love for him? Do you regularly tell him that you love him? Don't hesitate; he's all ears!

2. More than a thousand times the heart is mentioned in the Bible with regard to prayer. Can you put aside times to be with Jesus—to meet him at "the well"?

3. Will you pray to the Holy Spirit for guidance for your prayer life?

My Hands to Serve Him

1. At your particular state in life as a Catholic woman, what ways do you serve God in others? Can you list at least three?

2. Do you strive to see Jesus in others—your spouse, children, neighbors, coworkers, fellow religious? Do you serve Jesus in them? What steps can you take to be more aware of Jesus' presence within them? Can you list three examples?

How to Defend the Faith without Raising your voice

3. Do you feel God might be asking you to serve him con-
    cretely in a new way? If so, can you list a few ideas and
    then pray about the possibility?

Seeking God

Dear Lord Jesus, you are forever in search of my heart, even when
I turn my back on you. I am sorry for all of the times I have failed
to meet you at the well of prayer. I want to love you more. Thank
you for your love! Amen.

4. *O*FFERING ME LIVING WATER

Worship the Lord with gladness; come into
his presence with singing.

—Psalm 100:2

In the last chapter we reflected on the Samaritan woman
and Jesus' desire to meet us at the "well of prayer." In this
chapter we will consider the many forms of prayer and how
we can achieve peace of soul through prayer. St. Thérèse
of Lisieux wrote a beautiful morning prayer that expresses
how each day of our lives should be a prayer offered from
a heart in love with God:

> O my God! I offer thee all my actions of this day for the
> intentions and for the glory of the Sacred Heart of Jesus.
> I desire to sanctify every beat of my heart, my every
> thought, my simplest works, by uniting them to Its infi-
> nite merits; and I wish to make reparation for my sins
> by casting them into the furnace of Its Merciful Love. O
> my God! I ask of thee for myself and for those whom
> I hold dear, the grace to fulfill perfectly thy Holy Will,
> to accept for love of thee the joys and sorrows of this

passing life, so that we may one day be united together
in heaven for all Eternity. Amen.

"OUT OF THE DEPTHS I CRY TO YOU, O LORD"

St. James and St. Paul have exhorted us to pray "at all times"
(Eph 5:20 and 6:18) and to "pray without ceasing" (1 Thes
5:17). We might be intimidated by their words or simply
brush them aside as an unattainable aim, or at least one
that we can't worry about right now. But let's discuss the
possibility, as well as the vital necessity, of a prayer-filled
Christian life.

First things first—begin each day with a morning offering to get your day going in the right direction. After this,
it's important to schedule your prayer times. While we all
want our prayer to be spontaneous and sincere, we also
know that, if we don't actually pencil in time with God, that
"meeting" might never happen. I understand what it is to be
busy! If I don't schedule pauses in my work, I usually won't
be able to fit in the Rosary that I hoped to pray or that quiet
time of meditation I wanted to get in.

Sometimes it can be a bit (or a lot!) of a struggle. It might
require sacrifice to make time for prayer, for instance, to
take the time to stop at the church on the way home. Yet,
even those few moments with the Lord, wherever we spend
them, are very valuable and well worth the effort. Mother
Teresa said, "Real love requires sacrifice" and "Real loving
hurts." Do we love the Lord enough to make this sacrifice of
time for him? How would your husband, children, friends,
or coworkers feel if you didn't make any time to converse
with them? We shouldn't forget our Lord who is the One
who makes all of our other relationships possible.

Our Church teaches that "prayer cannot be reduced to the spontaneous outpouring of interior impulse: in order to pray, one must have the will to pray" (CCC 2650). We can't expect prayer to just *happen*. We *will* it to happen by planning times for prayer. And the Holy Spirit urges us to pray, offering us wonderful inspirations throughout our busy days.

Even Jesus (who is God!) saw a vital need to draw apart from crowds and hubbub going on to seek out his Father in heaven. He continuously prayed prior to significant moments of his mission during his public ministry. He always praised his Father and thanked him, taking the time to pause and be still in prayer.

Schedule time slots that will work best for you and be prepared for interruptions. Flexibility is of the essence! Always keep in mind that our Lord knows your heart and your desire to come close to him. If your schedule happens to get rearranged, it's usually due to caring for the others with whom he has surrounded you. And it would be wrong to neglect or ignore the needs around you to kneel down to pray. So, try your best to achieve a balance and don't worry! Your desire to pray will make it happen. No matter how and when it is—our Lord will be pleased.

You might be able to schedule a time early in the morning, before things get too busy to meet with our Lord after you've said your morning offering. Or maybe you're able to schedule praying the Angelus or a decade (or more) of the Rosary at lunchtime, possibly even before Jesus in the Blessed Sacrament if you're able to get to the church or chapel. You might want to meditate on the readings of the day at times that work for you. Perhaps nighttime, when all has settled down, is when you can finally draw closer to Jesus' feet to pour out your heart and listen to his words for you. Possibly, all of the above will work for you. Do your best to make prayer happen in your life—*will* it!

Origen (185–232) said, "He 'prays without ceasing' who
unites prayer to works and good works to prayer. Only in
this way can we consider as realizable the principal of praying without ceasing."[1] Cardinal John Henry Newman also
spoke about praying without ceasing:

> A man cannot really be religious one hour, and not reli-
> gious the next. We might as well say he could be in a
> state of good health one hour, and in bad health the next.
> A man who is religious, is religious morning, noon, and
> night; his religion is a certain character, a mold in which
> his thoughts, words, actions are cast, all forming parts
> of one and the same whole. He sees God in all things;
> every course of action he directs towards those spiritual
> objects which God has revealed to him; every occurrence
> of the day, every event, every person met with, all news
> which he hears, he measures by the standard of God's
> will. And a person who does this may be said almost
> literally to pray without ceasing; for, knowing himself
> to be in God's presence, he is continually led to address
> him reverently, whom he sets always before him, in the
> inward language of prayer and praise, of humble confes-
> sion and joyful trust.[2]

Before we get into the "how-to" of prayer, we might
ask ourselves, What exactly is prayer? The *Catechism* offers
us two wonderful quotations from the saints to describe
prayer. St. Thérèse said, "For me, prayer is a surge of the
heart; it is a simple look turned toward heaven; it is a cry of
recognition and of love, embracing both trial and joy." And
St. John Damascene expressed this so beautifully in these
words: "Prayer is the raising of one's mind and heart to God
or the requesting of good things from God" (*CCC* 2558–59).

Prayer primarily is a conversation with God. As we know from the words at the end of the Eucharistic Prayer, our prayer is always made to the Trinity.

> Through him [Christ], with him, and in him,
> O God, Almighty Father,
> in the unity of the Holy Spirit,
> all glory and honor is yours,
> for ever and ever.

Yet at the same time, we can pray to each person of the Trinity. And we can ask for the intercession of Mary, our Mother, along with that of all the angels and the saints. We may do that in a formal way with the prayer of the Church or in an informal way using our own words. When we are aware of God and we love him, we desire to speak with him. It only makes sense—we share our thoughts with him, we ask for his help and guidance, and we ask him to help us love him more. We come out of ourselves and our preoccupations, turn toward God, and offer ourselves to him, in unity with the angels and the saints.

And because a conversation is two sided, we don't talk *at* God; we talk *with* God. I think that sometimes we pray as if God were deaf. We should expect God to speak back to us. We might not always hear him, but we listen, we wait faithfully, and we trust and believe that he will speak to our hearts, guide us, and give us the grace we need to persevere in this life and to live in eternal happiness with him in heaven one day. St. Augustine said, "To seek God is to desire happiness; to find him is that happiness."

MODES OF PRAYER

Depending on God for all of her needs through prayer, St. Teresa of Avila said, "Lord, you know all things, can do all things, and you love me." She knew that, because God loved her (as he loves all of us, too) and knew what was best, he would certainly care for all of her needs. The depth and purpose of prayer is as simple as that, yet so profound at the same time. It is really a surrender of our hearts and wills to God.

Prayer is essential in the Christian life. The *Catechism* tells us,

> Prayer and the Christian life are inseparable, for they concern the same love and the same renunciation, proceeding from love; the same filial and loving conformity with the Father's plan of love; the same transforming union in the Holy Spirit who conforms us more and more to Christ Jesus; the same love for all men, the love with which Jesus has loved us. "Whatever you ask the Father in my name, he [will] give it to you. This I command you, to love one another." (CCC 2745)

The driving forces behind prayer are faith and the love of God. Love will overcome our times of dryness or even our laziness in prayer. Our perseverance in prayer will reap the rewards of heaven. St. Alphonsus Liguori tells us, "Those who pray are certainly saved; those who do not pray are certainly damned" (*Del gran mezzo dello preghiera*). Maybe we had better step up our prayer lives!

Naturally, not everyone prays in the same way. Some prefer to go to a quiet corner of their home, convent, chapel, or church to pray and meditate. Some have a specific prayer chair at home to sit, meditate, and ponder. Some like to use tangible items such as Rosary beads to focus on specific meditations and to ask for the intercession of the Blessed Mother while moving their fingers over the beads. One of the ways I love to pray is out in nature. God's creation really makes my heart soar. I look at the natural world and my heart starts praying in the outdoor "cathedral." God must have given me the gift of being appreciative of his great work. When I do my gardening, I lift my heart to God. When I take a walk, I usually pray my Rosary or at least unite myself to Jesus, Mary, the angels, and the saints. Each of us has our own individual prayer path inspired by the Holy Spirit, but we can and should be aided by the Church's recommendations.

The Church structures a way for the faithful to pray by offering a liturgical calendar and basic rhythms of prayer to prod us to "pray without ceasing." Specifically, Holy Mother Church says,

> The Tradition of the Church proposes to the faithful certain rhythms of praying to nourish continuous prayer. Some are daily, such as morning and evening prayer, grace before and after meals, the Liturgy of the Hours. Sundays, centered on the Eucharist, are kept holy primarily by prayer. The cycle of the liturgical year and its great feasts are also basic rhythms of the Christian's life of prayer. (CCC 2698)

Although each person is unique in her prayer style, there are three major expressions of prayer in Christian tradition in which we dwell in God's presence: vocal, meditative, and contemplative. All three forms are parallel in that they each require our composure of heart.

According to the *Catechism*, vocal prayer is "founded on the union of body and soul in human nature, associates the body with the interior prayer of the heart" (CCC 2742). We vocally pray (either mentally or aloud) when we express ourselves in heartfelt prayer. A fine example of vocal prayer is when Jesus taught his disciples the Our Father prayer. Jesus also modeled vocal prayer when praying the liturgical prayers of the synagogue, prayers of blessing aloud, and his prayers in the agony in the Garden of Gethsemani. Vocal prayer is the most assessable prayer to groups who pray together.

Meditation is a prayer that engages our thoughts, imagination, emotion, and desire. The *Catechism* says that meditation "is above all a quest. The mind seeks to understand the why and how of the Christian life, in order to adhere and respond to what the Lord is asking" (*CCC* 2705). During meditation, we are aided by spiritual writings or the readings of the day. We read them, ponder them, and enter into prayer asking God to teach us. We can even meditate on a holy icon or image. We enter into our hearts deeply, and we might be asking, "Lord, what do you want me to do?" And we listen.

There are countless methods of meditation. Father John A. Hardon counsels us, "Daily reflection on the mysteries of faith is indispensable to keep the faith, which means to keep the truth."[3] He encouraged the faithful to reflect and meditate each day with solid spiritual writings to aid us. This will keep our faith alive. And this can be achieved by even us busy women. We can retreat to our hearts and meditate even on the busiest of days. Take a breath, pause for even a second or a moment, ponder God's great love, imagine him near you, whisper a prayer to him—tell him you love him—and listen to him. Then, reality "taps us on the shoulder," and we get immersed once again in our work. Try to find spontaneous moments throughout your days to meditate, and schedule longer periods of time to meditate, too, when you can utilize spiritual readings to prompt your meditations. Amazing graces are waiting!

Contemplation is a prayer in which our attention is fixed on the Lord himself. It is a prayer accepted in humility and poverty because it is a gift and a grace. The Holy

Spirit inspires the soul to pray contemplatively. Meditation can be involved in this inner prayer. We seek Jesus, and in him, the Father, because we love him—we want to unite our hearts to him.

St. Teresa of Avila explained, "Contemplative prayer in my opinion is nothing else than a close sharing between friends; it means taking time frequently to be alone with him who we know loves us."[4]

The Church teaches, "Contemplative prayer is the simple expression of the mystery of prayer. It is a gaze of faith fixed on Jesus, an attentiveness to the Word of God, a silent love. It achieves real union with the prayer of Christ to the extent that it makes us share in his mystery" (CCC 2724).

No matter what form of prayer we pray, the most essential thing is that our hearts are deeply involved. Don't worry so much about the methodological stuff. Just pour out your heart to our Lord and contemplate his great love for you!

PRAYING WITH THE SACRAMENTS AND SCRIPTURE

The Eucharist is central to a Catholic's life. All throughout Church history, the Eucharist has been celebrated in response to our Lord's command, "Do this in remembrance of me." The Mass is a memorial of Jesus' sacrifice of offering his life on the Cross as an oblation to God for us, but it's even more than that. We were told by Jesus "to *do this* in memory of me"—to repeat his actions. This has been done all through the centuries down to our present day. Catholics believe that the bread and wine offered at Mass—through the miracle of transubstantiation, which is performed by the Holy Spirit through the hands of the priest—becomes the Body and Blood, soul, and divinity of Christ, "the bread of heaven" and "the cup of salvation." We have the privilege to share in this sacrifice and celebration by gathering together in our churches to worship at Mass where our prayer and our Lord's prayer are united. Through participation in Mass and reception of the Eucharist, God has provided continuous nourishment for our soul, mind, and will.

The *Catechism* explains,

> The Eucharist is the memorial of Christ's Passover, the making present and the sacramental offering of his unique sacrifice, in the liturgy of the Church which is his Body. . . . When the Church celebrates the Eucharist, she commemorates Christ's Passover, and it is made present: the sacrifice Christ offered once for all on the cross remains ever present. (*CCC* 1362, 1364)

Amazingly, the Eucharist, which is called the "source and summit of the Christian life" (*LG* 11), "is celebrated in communion with the whole Church in heaven and on earth, the living and the dead, and in communion with the pastors of the Church, the Pope, the diocesan bishop, his presbyterium and his deacons, and all the bishops of the whole world together with their Churches" (*CCC* 1354).

While we are united with the whole Church, the Mass fuels us with the grace we need as Catholic women—it feeds us. The Eucharist feeds us when we receive it in Holy Communion. Jesus who is called "the Bread of Life" has instructed us to eat of his body and drink of his blood. This spiritual nourishment continues through the Blessed Sacrament when we receive Jesus in Spiritual Communion (which can be done anywhere) and also when we worship and adore him in our visits to the Blessed Sacrament. St. Peter Julian Eymard, lover and preacher of the Blessed Sacrament, has said, "Eucharistic Adoration is the greatest act of holiness on earth."[5]

Father Hardon taught that, as we pray to Jesus in the Blessed Sacrament, he feeds our souls and nourishes our minds and wills: "In the mind, we need light; in the will we need strength." Further, Father Hardon impresses upon us in his writings that "it is this Truth and Way become Incarnate [Jesus] who is with us and near and available to us."[6]

We need only approach him in love and ask him to teach us. "Speak, for your servant is listening" (1 Sm 3:7–11). St. Peter Julian Eymard instructs,

> As we grow to know his voice better (in Adoration) and as our hearts become more sympathetic to him in emptying themselves of what is not him, our Lord manifests Himself in a clearer and more intimate manner. . . . He gives the soul a divine conviction which overshadows the light of human reason."[7]

We women can feel very weary and even battered by the constant expectations and demands of others and by the noisy culture in which we live. Our Lord calls us to himself. He has said, "Come to me, all you that are weary and are carrying heavy burdens, and I will give you rest" (Mt 11:28). His words should comfort our souls. His presence will give us a deep and abiding peace.

Jesus has given me an inexpressible peace each time I stop in the church or chapel to be with him, even when it's for a short while. Do endeavor to spend time with Jesus in the Blessed Sacrament whenever you can. No one can ease our pain and weariness like he can.

Each of us needs to have an interior conversion of heart. The great sacrament that brings us this conversion, as well as the peace that accompanies it, is Confession (also called the Sacrament of Penance or the Sacrament of Reconciliation). Thankfully, God gives us a new heart through this sacrament. The *Catechism* teaches us that "it is by faith and Baptism that one renounces evil and gains salvation, that is, the forgiveness of all sins and the gift of new life" (*CCC*

1427). Baptism is the first conversion of heart. The second is that we are always in need of purification moved by God's grace and a contrite heart. So, our conversion experience is ongoing. St. Ambrose explained the two conversions like this: "There are water and tears: the water of Baptism and the tears of repentance." As long as we are living here on earth, we will have opportunities for repentance. We need it. We have a loving and merciful God who offers it to us.

Our Church teaches that there are many forms of penance in the Christian life. We learn from scripture and the Fathers of the Church that three forms are emphasized: fasting, prayer, and almsgiving. We are encouraged to reconcile with our neighbor, be sorry for our sins, have concern for our neighbor's salvation, practice charity, and call on the intercession of the saints because this "covers a multitude of sins" (1 Pt 4:8). Further, we learn,

> Conversion is accomplished in daily life by gestures of reconciliation, concern for the poor, the exercise and defense of justice and right, by the admission of faults to one's brethren, fraternal correction, revision of life, examination of conscience, spiritual direction, acceptance of suffering, endurance of persecution for the sake of righteousness. Taking up one's cross each day and following Jesus is the surest way of penance. (CCC 1435)

In essence, taking up our crosses and allowing our Lord to do his work in us throughout all of the circumstances of our days is the perfect penance when we have surrendered our hearts and wills to God.

The scriptures are central to a Catholic's life. But when approaching the scriptures in prayer, there is no need to feel intimidated about whether or not we are doing it the right way. We are free to meditate on little bits of scripture piece by piece or the readings of each day. There is a specific type of ancient prayer called lectio divina (Latin for "divine reading"), which is a method of praying with scripture. Lectio divina is being rediscovered in our modern day. It involves reading, meditation, prayer, and contemplation, individually or in groups. Essentially, praying lectio divina is endeavoring to be in God's presence and entering into a dialogue with him by slowly reading and pondering a part of scripture (even one word) and offering your rumination to him.

Pope Benedict XVI spoke about scripture in *Verbum Domini* (*The Word of the Lord*).[8] In it, he highlights the fundamental role of "God the Father, source and origin of the Word"(*VD* 20) and the Trinitarian dimension of revelation. He speaks about "God's will to open and maintain a dialogue with man, in which God takes the initiative and reveals Himself in various ways" (*VD* 6). Pope Benedict tells us about the relationship of the Eucharist and tradition on the theme of inspiration and the truth of the Bible as well as "the duty of Christians to announce the Word of God in the world in which we live and work." Our Holy Father reaffirmed his exhortation to all Christians "to become increasingly familiar with Sacred Scripture."[9]

There are many ways we Catholic women can become more familiar with sacred scripture. We can read it more often, ponder it, study it within a group, and prayerfully meditate upon it. By reading the scriptures in the daily readings of each day we unite ourselves with the whole Church. Participating in daily Mass whenever possible is very valuable to us and brings us in touch with the scriptures as well.

And let's not forget "to announce the Word of God in the world in which we live and work" as Pope Benedict prodded us to do. If we *live* the scriptures by following God's design for our lives, we will be announcing them to all around us. We can bear in mind the words attributed to St. Francis of Assisi: "Preach the gospel at all times and when

necessary, use words." Most times we won't be shouting
scriptures from the rooftops, but we'll be *living* them, and
our example will reach out to all those around us. So, even
though we are urged by our Church to spread the gospels to
the ends of the earth, we might be spreading it to the ends
of our households, convents, and workplaces. That's where
it starts for sure.

One scripture I endeavor to live is a favorite of Blessed
Teresa's. It's the "judgment of the nations" in Matthew
25:31–46, when Jesus tells us, "Truly I tell you, just as you
did it to one of the least of these who are members of my
family, you did it to me." Blessed Mother Teresa often taught
the significance of that scripture by simply holding up one
of her hands and counting down on her five fingers, "You-
did-it-to-me!" We now have another way to view our hands.
Hopefully this will remind us to discover and serve Jesus
in others.

PRAYERFUL DEVOTIONS

There are numerous Catholic devotions, and I'll include a
few popular ones here: the Rosary, praying various chaplets,
devotion to the Sacred Heart of Jesus and the Immaculate
Heart of Mary, the Divine Mercy devotion and all sorts of
novenas.

In *Familiaris Consortio* (*The Role of the Christian Family
in the Modern World*), Blessed John Paul II underscored the
importance of private prayer and devotions by the family:

> As preparation for the worship celebrated in church,
> and as its prolongation in the home, the Christian family
> makes use of private prayer, which presents a great vari-
> ety of forms. While this variety testifies to the extraor-
> dinary richness with which the Spirit vivifies Christian
> prayer, it serves also to meet the various needs and life

situations of those who turn to the Lord in prayer. Apart from morning and evening prayers, certain forms of prayer are to be expressly encouraged, following the indications of the Synod Fathers, such as reading and meditating on the word of God, preparation for the reception of the sacraments, devotion and consecration to the Sacred Heart of Jesus, the various forms of veneration of the Blessed Virgin Mary, grace before and after meals, and observance of popular devotions. (*FC* 61)

Regarding the Sacred Heart of Jesus, we learn from the *Catechism*:

The prayer of the Church venerates and honors the *Heart of Jesus* just as it invokes his most holy name. It adores the incarnate Word and his Heart which, out of love for men, he allowed to be pierced by our sins. Christian prayer loves to follow the way of the cross in the Savior's steps. (*CCC* 2669)

Many Catholic homes, schools, convents, and rectories are adorned with at least one image of the Sacred Heart of Jesus somewhere on their walls. I have images in my dining room and also in the living room. I can't tell you how many times I have paused by or knelt in front of the images when in need or simply to pray to Jesus while in the comfort of my domestic church—my home.

In the quiet town of Paray le Monial in the center of France, over a period of seventeen years, Jesus appeared to St. Margaret Mary Alacoque (1670–1690), a Visitation nun to whom he revealed his Sacred Heart and gave directions for devotion to his heart. Today we know these as "First Friday Devotions."[10]

The Rosary, a wonderful form of meditation, is not just your grandmother's prayer. Though, I am very thankful that my grandmother, in praying the Rosary, set a fantastic example, which has stayed with me. The Rosary can be said by anyone and virtually anywhere. Basically, when praying the Rosary, one meditates on "mysteries" of joy, sorrow, glory, and light, recalling scriptural passages that mark the lives of Jesus and Mary.

Many of the saints have used this form of prayer and have highly recommended it to the faithful. Many popes throughout the centuries have encouraged this prayer as well. Pope Pius IX said, "Among all the devotions approved by the Church none has been so favored by so many miracles as the devotion of the Most Holy Rosary."

I have a special devotion to the Rosary and believe it to be a powerful prayer. I always have a Rosary in my pocket or purse. And if I am without my beads or unable to use them (when driving, folding laundry, etc.), I just use my ten fingers to count my decades of Hail Marys. I don't think our Lord or his Blessed Mother mind.

To offer a little background, the Rosary grew out of the practice of the laity praying 150 Hail Marys in imitation of the monks who prayed 150 psalms daily. This monastic practice is called the Divine Office (also known as the breviary or Liturgy of the Hours). The laity (some of whom couldn't read or obtain a copy of the Psalms) substituted Hail Marys for the Psalms. Some of the first rosaries were simply cords with knots tied along them to keep one's place and count the prayers.

The Church believes that the Blessed Mother herself asked for the practice of the Rosary to fight heresy and sin. The first reference we have to the Rosary is from St. Dominic (1170–1221), the founder of the Order of Preachers, who preached a form of the Rosary in France when the Albigensian heresy was attacking the faith. Our modern-day Rosary is said to have come from the time of Alan de Roche

(1428–1475), a disciple of St. Dominic's who promoted the Rosary by establishing Rosary confraternities.

When the Blessed Mother appeared at Fatima (an apparition approved by the Church), she said, "Say the Rosary every day to obtain peace for the world." Blessed John Paul II loved the prayer of the Rosary and highly recommended it to families. He called the Rosary his favorite prayer, after the Mass and the Liturgy of the Hours.[11]

The Divine Mercy devotion centers on God's great mercy and the Hour of Great Mercy (3:00 p.m.) when Jesus died on the Cross; it originated in the 1930s with St. Faustina Kowalska, a Polish nun who, in obedience to her spiritual director, wrote a six-hundred-page diary recounting revelations she received about God's mercy. Jesus appeared to Sister Faustina with rays radiating from his heart on February 22, 1931, and told her, "Paint an image according to the pattern you see, with the signature: Jesus I trust in you. I desire that this image be venerated, first in your chapel, and throughout the world."[12]

Jesus warned about his divine judgment; the *Catechism* explains, "On Judgment Day at the end of the world, Christ will come in glory to achieve the definitive triumph of good over evil which, like the wheat and the tares, have grown up together in the course of history" (*CCC* 681).

Jesus told Sister Faustina, "Speak to the world about My mercy. . . . It is a sign for the end times. After it will come the Day of Justice. While there is still time, let them have recourse to the fountain of My mercy."[13]

Jesus asked Sister Faustina that a feast day be dedicated to Divine Mercy and specified that it should be the Sunday after Easter Sunday. Jesus told her, "Whoever approaches the Fountain of Life on this day will be granted complete forgiveness of sins and punishment."[14]

In a decree dated May 23, 2000, the Congregation for Divine Worship and the Discipline of the Sacraments stated that "throughout the world the Second Sunday of Easter will receive the name Divine Mercy Sunday, a perennial invitation to the Christian world to face, with confidence in divine benevolence, the difficulties and trials that mankind will experience in the years to come."

Many Catholics are devoted to praying the Divine Mercy chaplet (usually at 3:00 p.m.) which can be said on ordinary Rosary beads and in which prayers are said to invoke God's mercy on us and on the whole world.[15]

INVOKING HEAVENLY INTERCESSION

In addition to praying to God and the Blessed Trinity, we can prayerfully invoke the Blessed Mother, the angels, and the saints as heavenly intercessors. Angels are pure spirits who were created by God before the human race. They are intelligent, pure beings and have no bodies but are like us in that they have a mind and a will. Their purpose is to serve our needs. Father Hardon says, "They are literally the guardians of the human race."[16]

We are each blessed to have our own guardian angel. What a privilege! Father Hardon explains:

> The angels are providential intermediaries between God, whose vision they already enjoy, and mankind, whom they are entrusted to lead to the vision not yet attained. We therefore have not only the privilege but the duty to talk with the angels in easy, intimate and frequent conversations.[17]

Let's be sure to keep company with the angels. Doesn't that sound like such an amazing privilege?

Of course, we know that Mary, Jesus' mother, is highly favored by God and a wonderful intercessor for us women. She knows what we are all about. It's wise to call upon her for her help throughout our daily lives. One way to remain in conversation with the Blessed Mother is through the Rosary. There are numerous other prayers to the Blessed Mother that can be said as well (for example, the Memorare). Of course, your informal conversations with her are indeed special and welcomed by her.

Another huge part of that invisible world is the saints— those who have gone before us and are marked by the sign of faith. Some have been beatified or canonized by the Church, and some are unknown who are part of the great Communion of Saints (as are we).

The Church encourages us to call upon the saints for assistance.

> It is not merely by the title of example that we cherish the memory of those in heaven. We seek rather that by this devotion to the exercise of fraternal charity the union of the whole Church in the Spirit may be strengthened. Exactly as Christian communion between people on their earthly pilgrimage brings us closer to Christ, so our communion with the saints joins us to Christ from whom as from its fountain and head issues all grace and the very life of the people of God. (*LG* 50)

I call upon the saints for help each and every day. I have some favorites, but I love them all. Once when I was praying, I suddenly realized that someday I would actually meet and keep company face-to-face with my dear saint friends in heaven. That realization made my heart soar. The saints can help us immensely on our own personal journeys. Their example speaks volumes, and their intercession is powerful.

Consider as you pray to them for their help that they are continuously beholding the face of God. Get to know them.

LIVING IN THE PRESENCE OF GOD

We live in the presence of God by sincerely loving God in everything we do. St. Teresa of Avila said, "Settle yourself in solitude, and you will come upon him in yourself." It doesn't matter how busy we are because the numerous occupations that fill our daily lives won't hinder the prayer of our hearts. Father Hardon says, "These duties are precisely God's way of providing us with opportunities for putting our prayer of the heart into practice."[18] He means we can pray throughout everything.

I wholeheartedly believe that God allows us umpteen opportunities for his grace each day. All of the challenges and frustrations we face can be beneficial occasions to turn to God and ask for his grace for ourselves and for the people we are dealing with. No matter what is happening around us and within us, we always have recourse to prayer. Prayer is a gift that can never be taken from us. As long as we are conscious (and even if not our our hearts may be praying), whatever is happening in our lives, we always—and I mean always—have recourse to prayer.

Let's not forget about prayerful "aspirations" as part of our prayer repertoire. An aspiration is a prayer that arises spontaneously from the heart, expressing love to our Creator or crying out in need. It can simply be in our loving words or in a traditional formula. We can call upon the angels and saints this way as well. Once when my twenty-year-old daughter Mary-Catherine was studying abroad in France, I happened to call her cell phone right as a man was stalking her. She had been dodging him by getting off at a different stop of the metro route to trick him so he wouldn't be able to follow her further. It worked and so did the prayers. Being 3,532 miles away, prayer was my only recourse at that moment. "Oh, Lord, please protect her! Blessed Mother Mary, help! Guardian angel, protect her!" Sometimes that's what a mother's prayer sounds like.

Then there are the aspirations of prayer at calmer times. For example, "O, Mary, conceived without sin, pray for us who have recourse to thee" (these words appear on the Miraculous Medal). There are so many beautiful aspirations. I suggest you select a few and commit them to memory.

- Blessed be God!

- Blessed be the name of the Lord!

- Divine Heart of Jesus, convert sinners, save the dying, deliver the holy souls in purgatory.

- Eucharistic Heart of Jesus, increase in us our faith, hope, and charity.

- Good Jesus, give me a deep love for thee, that nothing may be too hard for me to bear from thee.

- Heart of Jesus, burning with love for us, set our hearts on fire with love of thee.

- Heart of Jesus, I put my trust in thee!

- Jesus, I trust in you!

- Jesus, meek and humble of heart, make our hearts like unto thine.

- Jesus, my God, I love thee above all things!

- Jesus, Son of David, have mercy on me!

- May the most just, most high, and most adorable will of God be done in all things, praised and magnified forever.

- My God and my all.

- My Jesus, mercy!

- My Lord Jesus Christ, for the sake of thy sufferings, grant me such faith, hope, charity, sorrow for my sins, and love of prayer as will save and sanctify my soul.

- My Lord, grant that I may love thee, and that the reward of my love may be to love thee ever more and more.

- My sweetest Jesus, be not my Judge, but my Savior.

- Good Jesus, shelter me from the evil one, shed thy dew upon me to calm my soul, and dwell in me fully, that I may wholly love thee.

- Good Jesus, my God and my All, keep me ever near thee, let nothing for a moment separate me from thee.

- Praised be Jesus Christ, now and forevermore.

- Sacred Heart of Jesus, thy kingdom come!

- Savior of the world, have mercy on us.

- Sweet Heart of Jesus, be my love!

- Sweet Heart of my Jesus, grant that I may ever love thee more.

- We adore and praise thee, most holy Lord Jesus Christ, because by Thy holy cross Thou hast redeemed the world.

Jesus in the Blessed Sacrament

- Jesus, my God, here present in the Sacrament of thy love, I adore thee.

- Jesus in the Blessed Sacrament, have mercy on us.

- Jesus, in the most holy Sacrament, have mercy on us.

- Praised and adored forever be the most holy Sacrament.

- We adore thee, thou true Bread of angels.

Blessed Mother Mary

- Mary, Virgin Mother of God, pray to Jesus for me.
- Sweet Heart of Mary, be my salvation!
- Mary, conceived without sin, pray for us who have recourse to thee.
- Our Lady of Lourdes (or Fatima or Guadalupe) pray for us!
- Mary, our hope, have pity on us!
- Mary, most sorrowful, Mother of Christians, pray for us.
- Mary, virgin Mother of God, pray to Jesus for me.
- My Queen! My Mother! Remember I am thine own. Keep me, guard me, as thy property and possession.
- Mary, thou didst enter the world without stain; do thou obtain for me from God, that I may leave it without sin.

The Holy Family

- Jesus, Mary, Joseph!
- Jesus, Mary, and Joseph, bless us now and at the hour of our deaths.
- Jesus, Mary, and Joseph, I give you my heart and my soul. Jesus, Mary, and Joseph, assist me in my last agony. Jesus, Mary, and Joseph, may I breathe out my soul in peace with you.

I so often simply say, "Jesus!" or "Jesus, I love you!" I also often say a short aspiration Mother Teresa taught me: "Mary, Mother of Jesus, be a mother to me now."

OFFERING UP OUR SUFFERINGS AND DAILY DUTIES

A possibly much overlooked form of prayer is "offering it up." This means offering up our sufferings and being faithful to our daily duties. Many of the saints understood the importance in offering up their daily duties to God so that he could use them as he wills. We need to keep in mind that Jesus has told us, "If any want to become my followers, let them deny themselves and take up their cross and follow me" (Mt 16:24).

Picking up our "crosses" could mean offering our daily duties to God with love and accepting what he gives us each day—challenges and all. This all goes back to the practice of praying a morning offering each day, which I spoke about earlier. In that amazing prayer, we offer up our prayers, works, joys, and sufferings to God in advance of our day ahead.

St. Bernadette Soubirous was assigned very menial tasks to do in the convent, including mopping the floors and cleaning toilets, even though she had been chosen by the Blessed Mother to receive visits from her at Lourdes. The mother superior was very hard on Sister Bernadette and didn't seem to care that she was chosen by God to receive apparitions in Lourdes, France. Sister Bernadette would pray and offer up the work, doing each task with diligence and love for the Lord. She was laughed at by her fellow nuns because she cleaned the toilets. And, though it was difficult, she offered it all up to God so he would sanctify it all according to his holy will. These sorts of offerings are the stuff that makes saints.

This reminds me of the time Blessed Teresa came out of a bathroom at one of her convents smiling from ear to ear. One of the sisters asked why she was so happy and she said something to the effect, "Some sister here really loves our Lord. The bathroom is sparkling clean!" Mother Teresa knew that the sister must have been doing her menial task with great love. You see, nothing is *menial* or *small* to our Lord. Everything we do counts for something, and when done with love and gratitude our Lord is pleased. Not everyone will consider cleaning toilets a noble task. But if we search our hearts and are constant in prayer, we will understand that each thing we do can be a prayer to God. Perhaps you can take some time to consider this form of prayer.

Since we are talking about struggles, I want to be sure to mention that sometimes our prayers will simply be like an inner groaning of our spirit. We might be suffering so much that we can't really articulate our prayers, so instead we just *offer*—we offer our pain and our weakness to God—we give him our hearts. He knows. "Likewise the Spirit helps us in our weakness; for we do not know how to pray as we ought, but that very Spirit intercedes with sighs too deep for words. And God, who searches the heart, knows what is the mind of the Spirit, because the Spirit intercedes for the saints according to the will of God" (Rom 8:26–27). At those times when you can't pray, just close your eyes and love God.

When we are sick, challenged, upset, worn down, or suffering in some way, we can offer those feelings to God and ask him to sanctify our offerings and grant us graces for ourselves and the people to whom we serve or minister. We should do so with love and without complaints. It's okay to ask God for help to endure the situations, of course. He wants us to ask. It's also fine to ask if he can take them away—to heal us. But whatever I am going through, he knows. I consider him the Divine Physician who knows exactly what I need and when I need it. We have to trust him, and we shouldn't "waste" our suffering.

Many of the saints spoke about being faithful to their daily duties as the real road to holiness. It might sound absurd that just doing our daily grind can get us to heaven, but it can! The key is to do our tasks faithfully and prayerfully. Remember, St. Bernadette didn't complain when given the chore of scrubbing the toilets. She knew it was what God wanted for her—to be faithful to it. We don't have to know necessarily that God wants it—but we accept it and even try to do so with joy or at least a good dose of acquiescence.

St. Francis de Sales said that difficult and unpleasant tasks can become enjoyable and even easy when done with love. In his preaching he used an analogy of bees gathering the bitter nectar of thyme and converting it into sweet honey. He said, "Similarly, Christians undoubtedly find bitterness in their mortifications, but in performing them they change them into sweetness itself."[19]

If you are a mother, being faithful to your daily duties means to mother your children to the best of your ability and with as much love as possible. If you are a chef, show up to work on time (or even a little early) and make the best food you possibly can. If you are a teacher, be the best teacher possible and an exemplary example to your students and beyond.

I know these examples might seem oversimplified, but I chose them purposely to say that we need to be faithful to our duties in life—whatever they are. We should not be slackers; we should be on time, be attentive, be faithful and loving, and *really* care about what we are doing. We should do everything we do to give glory to God. We can do so even if we are sick in bed.

There is also a world of technology if we are inclined to use it in prayer. While it might feel a bit awkward to pull out your smart phone during Eucharistic Adoration, I know priests, religious, and the laity who use the apps during prayer, even in front of the Blessed Sacrament. I have a few of these sorts of applications on my devices and enjoy having access to them while traveling and even when at home. They can be great prayer aids. One, for instance, is comprised of images of each Station of the Cross that can be meditated upon when one isn't able to get to the church or chapel. Others have the readings of the day or the mysteries of the Rosary, and much more.

One evening when writing this book, I got a call from a friend who wanted to tell me how thankful she was for my prayers for her and her daughters during the past few years while she went through a very tough divorce. At times, I prayed for her right over the phone when she felt very troubled and scared. It brought her peace. Even though she had been away from the Church for many years, one time when we met for a short visit, I handed her my blessed Rosary beads and told her to keep them and just hold them when she felt troubled and to pray to the Blessed Mother.

My friend told me that the Rosary helped her immensely and that she and her daughters held it when they felt troubled. She told me that night she called, "If I didn't hold on to those beads, I don't know if I would have made it. Every so often when I was out, I would just stop at the church and go in and pray . . . it changed my life." She felt a great deal of comfort from the Rosary beads, a wonderful sacramental of our Church. She felt very connected to the Church, even though she was not actively going to Mass on a regular basis. She knew I was praying for her.

That night she told me that she was finding her way back to the Church and will be enrolling her daughters in the religious education program at the Catholic parish in her town as well as getting her youngest daughter baptized after putting it off for many years. Prayer changes things! We mustn't forget that.

A MOMENT TO REFLECT

After all this talk about kinds of prayer, possibly it all boils down to one thing: the true benefit of prayer is to get us to heaven! Of course, it's much more than that, but that is indeed the end result of a life of prayer. St. John Chrysostom tells us, "Nothing is equal to prayer; for what is impossible it makes possible, what is difficult, easy. . . . For it is impossible, utterly impossible, for the man who prays eagerly and invokes God ceaselessly ever to sin" (CCC 2744). I also love what St. Dominic Savio has said: "Nothing seems tiresome or painful when you are working for a Master who pays well; who rewards even a cup of cold water given for love of him."[20] Certainly, these are comforting words to take to our hearts.

Remember that prayer is a special treasure that resides in your heart and that no one can take from you—no matter what.

My Mind to Know Him

1. Since prayer can sometimes be a struggle, what concrete steps can you take to make it happen more often—to *will* it? List three ideas.

2. What can you do to stimulate your mind regarding learning more about prayer? Can you possibly "unplug" from some technology today, or soon, to be more attentive to hear God's "voice" in your life?

3. Set aside some time soon to research a bit about the saints and some of their prayer habits.

My Heart to Love Him

1. To love God, we don't use only our hearts but also our minds and senses. What are some ways you love God?

2. Are you willing to try a new form of prayer (approved by the Church), perhaps one that was mentioned in this chapter such as meditation on scriptures?

3. Sometime this week, can you read a section of the *Catechism* regarding prayer?

My Hands to Serve Him

1. Who in your life do you serve with God's love? Have you spoken to that person (or people) about prayer? Are you an example of prayer to them?

2. Today when you serve those around you with Christ's love, be sure to smile. A simple smile can have a huge impact in someone's life. It can also lighten your own mood.

3. Say a prayer before and during your challenging tasks. Ask God to guide you through it and shine through you to others.

Seeking God

Dear Lord, Jesus, open my heart and soul to hear you speaking to me. Teach me to pause and ponder your great Love for me so that, with your grace, I may pass it on to others. Amen.

PART THREE

CHRIST IS MY LIFE

Do not be conformed to this world, but be transformed by the renewing of your minds, so that you may discern what is the will of God—what is good and acceptable and perfect.

—Romans 12:2

5. *I*N MY HOME

The wise woman builds her house.

—Proverbs 14:1

One late afternoon, when driving home from doing errands with my young children, they all clamored from the backseat that they wanted to go out to eat. Even though I am half Polish, with some Irish and Scottish, and a bit of American Indian, I mustered up the best Spanish accent I could and said, "How about we go to 'La Hacienda?'" I could see smiles broaden across their faces in the rear-view mirror. They were enthused at the idea, that is, until we pulled into the driveway. That's when I quickly defined "La Hacienda" and explained that we couldn't go out to dinner that night and that our home was a very nice place to be.

Our home is not merely our dwelling place—it is a part of us. Most of us can recollect our family memories—both the happy and the not-so-pleasant ones. I'll never forget the story Mother Teresa told about the little girl her sisters had taken in and cared for. After a few days she went missing. The sisters searched for her and finally found her under a tree with her mother and siblings. Her home was with her mother and family even though their food was sparse and the tree was their only shelter—love kept her nurtured.

How is Christ *my life* at home? How can I discover him there? Well, truth be told, he is right there with us amid the joys and challenges of each day, even when we are not cognizant of him. Yet we *can* strive to find him even between the pots, pans, and busyness of family life.

As a Catholic mother, for me, the greatest joy in my vocation is in the awareness that I have been raising my five children in the faith all these years—thirty-five to be exact. I consider my home to be a "domestic church," a little church where amazing growth and transformation happens right within the nitty-gritty details of daily life—those ordinary moments that actually aren't quite so ordinary.

Catholic mothers work out their own and their family's salvation by living the theological virtues of faith, hope, and love every day in the home. Naturally, our spiritual lives are a work in progress, as is our family's. We make mistakes at times. We're not saints yet! When we've messed up, we dust ourselves off and ask for forgiveness and grace to continue putting one foot in front of the other every day to fulfill our Christian obligations in leading our family on the narrow path that leads to heaven. As we do, all of our efforts will reap many blessed benefits as well as provide us many occasions to sacrifice and pray even more for our children.

The *Catechism* tells us:

> The Christian family constitutes a specific revelation and realization of ecclesial communion, and for this reason it can and should be called a *domestic church*. It is a community of faith, hope, and charity; it assumes singular importance in the Church, as is evident in the New Testament. (CCC 2204)

After welcoming life in the family, the parents are gravely responsible and privileged with the raising of their children in the faith. The Church emphasizes this when teaching that parents "bear witness to this responsibility first by *creating a home* where tenderness, forgiveness, respect, fidelity, and disinterested service are the rule" (*CCC* 2223).

Let's keep those key words "creating a home" in mind. For, we *create* our domestic churches with God's help. It doesn't just happen by itself. One of the first things my husband Dave said to me when we were courting was, "A house is just four walls until the woman makes it a home." Proverbs also teaches us, "The wise woman builds her house" (Prv 14:1). Throughout this chapter we'll talk about how she accomplishes that.

The Church places great importance on the family unit. After all, the family is the "original cell of social life" (*CCC* 2207). We might not be totally aware of this fact given the state of affairs of our society in our day. But the Church upholds the dignity of the family and maintains that the family is

> the natural society in which husband and wife are called to give themselves in love and in the gift of life. . . . The family is the community in which, from childhood, one can learn moral values, begin to honor God, and make good use of freedom. Family life is an initiation into life in society. (*CCC* 2207)

Considering how the stable family is supposed to initiate its children into society after raising them with Christian values, it's no wonder that crime is out of control in our society today. So many children have not experienced a healthy and wholesome upbringing and a family life that is necessary to initiate them properly into society.

There are many different kinds of family units in our day: traditional two-parent families, single-parent families, grandparents or aunts and uncles raising the children, foster families, step-families, and adoptive families. My own domestic church has taken on many different shapes and forms over the years, not only because I have moved around but also because for many years my domestic church was a single-parent household. Through it all Christ was indeed there with us, at the center of our lives.

Through thick and thin Catholic parents should, in the spirit of self-denial, self-mastery, and sound judgment, help mold their children's consciences, schooling them in the virtues throughout their days. I'm sure you know what I mean by "thick and thin." We help raise our little saints to heaven right in the trenches of family life, during their sibling squabbles, our sleepless nights, and the various growing pains, difficulties, and of course the heartwarming milestones of family life. Everything in the family becomes an opportunity for great grace when we respond to it with love.

In the Heart of My Home

If you were to visit my home you would probably notice that in addition to the scores of family photos all over the place (I can't help it; I'm a mother!), it is adorned with numerous religious images and icons throughout. Over the years, I've tried my best to make God more tangible to my children and to create a spiritual atmosphere at home so it was a true *domestic church*. I wanted our family to think of God and ponder his love even while occupied in routine things.

I made sure that our Lord, his Mother, and the saints were at home with us—and not just their images. Our domestic church exuded spirituality amid the chaos of family life. And all of those tangible reminders I placed around my home are like sparks of faith for all of us who observe them—family, visitors, neighbors, delivery people, and everyone who walks through the door. God works through the icons and images to pull us closer to him.

All of this doesn't mean that life in my family on any given day will meticulously resemble a page out of the *Catechism*—maybe far from it! But I do strive to mirror God's love each day and foster a prayerful atmosphere at home, even as the kids are now moving into adulthood.

What I am trying to say is that we can't expect perfection in the family this side of heaven. Our halos aren't sparkling yet! So you can take that pressure off yourself right now. We, of course, never stop teaching our families and striving to be beautiful, loving Christian examples to our families and beyond—all with God's incredible grace!

Speaking of falling short of our intentions at times, I am reminded of when my coteacher, Jeanne, needed me to give her a ride home one evening after teaching a religious education class. She had locked her key in her car. I was happy to oblige, but instant visions of my messy car flashed in my brain. I had been so busy that I had not had time to tidy it up in a while. I apologized in advance, and Jeanne told me that she imagined my car would have been "sparkling clean" but was happy that it wasn't because it made me seem "more human" in her eyes. Good thing she didn't need to stop at my house, too! Again, we are not perfect creatures, and what truly matters is that our hearts are in the right place with God.

The areas of her home a Catholic mother should concentrate on are first and foremost her spouse and children's well-being, happiness, and spiritual and physical nourishment. She'll want to "build her house" with love. She'll be sure to create an atmosphere of pervading love and prayer. She'll work on her own prayer life, teach her children to establish their individual prayer lives, and make a point of praying together with the family at specific times. She helps her children to discover Christ at home in their domestic church as well as at the church building.

A Catholic mom wants her home to feel warm and inviting. She wants her family to feel comfortable and loved. They come first. As I've repeated many times, Mother Teresa often preached, "Love begins at home." So, we don't want to get our priorities confused and join all kinds of committees trying to do our ministry work to help the "world" unless our families are taken care of first. We certainly don't want to inadvertently neglect someone's needs.

My husband, Dave, and I know a couple who live in a very sterile-looking home. The husband doesn't permit his wife to have knick-knacks and scoffs at the idea every time she tries to bring a little bric-a-brac in to decorate their sparse house. The husband, being handy with woodwork and such, installed a chrome-colored, diamond-plate piece of metal in the middle of the kitchen floor! That's his style. Diamond plate is what you might see at industrial loading docks and sometimes at railroad crossings. His wife has sadly been prevented from "feathering her nest," as my husband likes to describe it. But now that they have two children, I think he'll start to see some changes in his previously barren house. Mothers need to feather their nests. It's what we do.

Sunday

I remarked to Dave one evening that it just did not seem like a Sunday. It was a fairly quiet day, and we participated in a beautiful Mass that morning, but something didn't seem right. After just a few minutes of thinking about it, I realized what it was. Both of us had put in a chunk of time at our work. I was busy working to meet a looming deadline for a writing project, and my husband had gone to his shop where he operates his business to finish up a pressing job. It was only about a three-hour period of working time that afternoon, but it really seemed to throw the whole day off. We seldom do our work on Sunday, but once in a while our schedules demand it.

Sunday in the Catholic home should be a day to enjoy together in the family. It can be a real challenge to make that happen in our media-driven, overly packed lives—to actually pause to enjoy—but it's essential, and God wants it. When I was growing up, I always knew when it was Sunday. We went to Mass, had a pancake breakfast and a big meal in the afternoon, and kicked back a bit. We usually visited our relatives, or they stopped by to see us. In addition to participating in the holy Mass together, which is the heart of the Church's life, the Church tells us that families should refrain from unnecessary work to allow time for rest, to be together, and to show Christian charity to others when possible.

As wonderful and ideal as it would be to relax and not worry about getting extra things done on a Sunday, like catching up with housework that couldn't be completed during a busy workweek, the reality for some women is that it is the only time to do so. If this is the case, endeavor to find even a short quiet time to do some spiritual reading to accentuate the Sunday, or take a moment to reach out by phone or e-mail to someone in need. Try to make Sunday dinnertime special and possibly do something fun together as a family, like taking a walk together, watching a movie, or playing a game.

The third commandment speaks of the holiness of Sunday. And in the Psalms we read, "This is the day that the Lord has made; let us rejoice and be glad in it" (Ps 118:24). It might not seem like the holiest of days when you consider how mall parking lots are jam-packed and church parking lots seem a bit less crowded. The Church admits that it takes a common effort to observe Sundays properly. For instance, the *Catechism* states, "Every Christian should avoid making unnecessary demands on others that would hinder them from observing the Lord's Day" (*CCC* 2187). Holy Mother Church acknowledges that some people need to work on Sundays, for example, the medical professionals, restaurant workers, public and social service people, and so on. You can read more about what the Church says about the meaning of Sunday in the *Catechism*.

The Church speaks of the wisdom of a day of rest: "The institution of Sunday helps all to 'be allowed sufficient rest and leisure to cultivate their familial, cultural, social, and religious lives'" (*CCC* 2194).

Are we Catholic mothers adhering to the Church's instructions in this regard? Are we allowing the family to do unnecessary shopping on Sundays or filling their day with anything but rest and family time? Do we encourage spiritual reading, decent movies, and wholesome games at home as well as family activities and time with relatives away from home? Let's ponder what we can do to reclaim the wisdom in keeping Sundays holy and restful.

The Kitchen

Back to my own home, I consider the real heart of my home to be my kitchen. It's the place we gather as a family and where I cook the meals I serve to my loved ones. It's the place that relatives and friends seem to plunk down when visiting rather than in the living room (even after I've spent a good deal of time tidying up that room!). Kitchens are warm, comfortable, and inviting. I have always loved my kitchen, whether it was the tiny one when I lived in an apartment or the larger one in my home now (even though it needs some cosmetic work).

I like to meet Jesus in my kitchen in the mornings. Now that my youngest is in college, the house is quiet (too quiet!). Well, my dog and two cats can keep things a bit lively. But on those quiet mornings, when Mary-Catherine is at school and Dave is already at work, instead of bringing my breakfast to my computer when I am itching to get going on my writing work, after I say grace, I sit at my kitchen table and gaze through the slider doors at the birds, trees, sky, and the sunshine streaming down. Or, weather permitting, go out on the deck to eat. I give glory to God and keep company with him while I eat. He speaks to my heart. I could have missed (and I many times do) the opportunity had I run up to my office and dove straight into work.

I have a thing about cooking for my family and cooking *with* them—creating healthy foods and fond memories, making a mess, laughing, and enjoying one another's company. It's so much the center of family life and should be—not the television or computer. I usually pray and ponder while chopping up the many vegetables that go into my soups and meals. It's a meditative time for me, for sure.

FAMILY DINNER

Families need to make the time to break bread together and share their thoughts and their hearts at the dinner table. Too many things and allurements in our world pull families away from their homes. It's essential to do everything within our power to ensure that family dinners do indeed occur and on a regular basis. That might mean cutting back on crazy schedules regarding sports practices, after-school and evening activities, and even church meetings, so that you can rediscover (if it's slipped away from you) that precious thing called "family dinner."

Naturally, we want our children to be well rounded, and sometimes that means allowing their involvement in sports and activities that often take place in the evenings. As parents we must keep an eye on the amount of activities they participate in, what it all entails, and how it impacts our family's life. In essence, we strive to find a healthy balance.

Countless American parents have become slaves to evening chaos regarding their children's sports activities that are not so family friendly. They often cause the family to be out of the home late into the night, to be running around and missing a healthy sit-down dinner. We need to move away from fast food and get back to *slow food* and dinner conversation. In addition to the problems caused by chaotic schedules, I really believe that family dinners are becoming more and more obsolete in many households and that family conversations have become a lost art. Many families I know, when they're not running around to evening sports practices and meetings, are grabbing fast food and takeout and eating their dinners in their car, in front of the television or computer, or at different times from one another. It's crazy!

There's added stress when the whole family lives this way and the kids grow up without a sense of togetherness, celebration, or peaceful evenings. No one gets enough sleep when there is still homework to begin after all the activities outside the house are finished. We know that a lack of sleep can cause illness, low productivity, and other problems, too—a vicious cycle.

Don't let the idiotic culture dictate to you your family schedule. Take a stand and bring back family dinners—start planning pleasant dinnertimes in your home, and rekindle precious time you can enjoy together. Hang a dry-erase board in the kitchen, and post the schedule for the family.

Having a pretty good idea of the evening activities a week in advance will help you to plan your meals accordingly. Do all you can to cut back or get rid of the evening-out schedule completely so that your family can enjoy one another's company at home, and get into a healthy rhythm. Is it time to take out the old board games?

Grandparents too have an integral role in their grandchildren's lives. If your children's children are caught up in overbooked schedules that don't allow for regular family dinners, perhaps you can find some way to help in this regard by encouraging get-togethers and occasionally having them at your home for dinner. Anything that keeps the family intact can help.

Let's also make sure that the kids aren't bringing all their devices to the dinner table. That goes for parents, too! In some cases, parents seem to have a constant need to check e-mails or status updates on their smart phones. We seem to have become slaves to little dings and sounds that alert us to e-mails and texts! It's tough enough to gather everyone together to eat because of our demanding schedules; it's even harder when competing with our overuse of technology. Devise rules for family time in the evenings—everyone is expected to the table on time, without the gadgets. Try to be sure homework is completed early enough so you can enjoy time together and have ample time for everyone to settle down before going to bed.

I've spent a good deal of time on the family dinner, and that's because I feel it is very central to family life. I believe that if more families were spending time together having dinner and conversing, our world would be a whole lot better.

I'd like to tell you a little story about my mother. It's a bit sad, but I think we can all learn from it. When my mother was in the hospital being treated for cancer, out of the blue she announced one day that when she got back home she was going to take out her good china and start using it. No more waiting for a special occasion. But my mother didn't make it back home to her house to celebrate with her fine china and fancy dishes. Instead, she went home to her eternal reward. Life really does speed by even when we're not faced with devastating and fatal illnesses. Please give some thought to adding a bit of pizzazz and celebration to your meals together. Make it special, and create your memories.

Amazing things really do happen when spending time in the heart of the home (hopefully unplugged from technology). We indeed forge a blessed familial bond together in the ordinariness of life. All of those "little" moments count—a lot! Throughout it all, we discover Christ at home with us.

A Vocation to the Single Life

Being single is another state of life for Catholic women. Some women are single because they never married, some are single because they are not yet married, and others because they don't feel a calling to marriage or the religious life. For single women, home life might involve living with their family or roommates, or living on their own. Like other lay faithful, single women carry out their vocation in the midst of the world.

Single women might have a special calling to ministry or to discern a vocation. They are not bound to the family or to a religious order so they have the flexibility to lend a hand to service in the Church and community as well as the ability to get involved with professions that require much time and dedication, such as the medical profession and education.

Lindsey Simmons, a prayerful and ambitious thirty-year-old single woman, told me, "Being single really allowed me ample time to discern a vocation and to indulge in the things I enjoy, such as reading, exercising, and traveling on a whim. One of my favorite things to do is curl up with a good book and allow myself to get lost for hours and hours—something that's hard to do when you are busy trying to foster a relationship or raising children as a mother!"

She feels blessed to have had time to ponder interests and her vocation while unattached. She said, "Singlehood also allows you time to discover what it is you enjoy, because you can try anything! When I was single and unattached, I really enjoyed being open to wherever the Spirit would move me next, and I know that the possibilities for a single person are endless."

She shared with me about her deep inner convictions. "I believe that we can live our faith every day," she said, "by being the hands of Christ here on earth." Lindsey certainly practices what she preaches. Her ministry repertoire has included volunteering at her local soup kitchen, serving on her parish stewardship committee, reaching out through a church prison ministry, praying outside of a local abortion clinic, and taking a mission trip to Puerto Rico. She absolutely loves being a Catholic and says she particularly loves the universality of the Church. "If you're looking," she said, "you can find signs of Christ and his Church everywhere, which I find very comforting."

Lindsey expressed that being a single Catholic woman does indeed have its challenges, though. "I do think that people expect marriage to be a natural and normal progression in life, so when someone isn't married, they immediately wonder why. *Doesn't she want to be married? If not, why? Is she looking for a husband? Doesn't she like kids and want a family?*

She continued, "I think that Catholics often think it's either marriage or the convent, which also isn't the case—many people are called to the vocation of single life, as well as the consecrated single life." Dealing with these notions can be tough for a single woman who is not yet sure of her vocation or is being called to a single vocation that others just don't understand. But Lindsey looks at the bright side. "I look at these various challenges that stem from our culture and my work and home life as ways God is shaping me, molding me, and preparing me for the future," she concluded.

There are other challenges for some single women as well. Lindsey shared, "Sometimes I feel like the world is set up to work more easily for married people, even though not everyone is called to that life." Single life can be hard and exhausting for women like Lindsey who own their own home and don't have the support of a spouse, as well as for others who are struggling financially or in other ways.

"Sometimes I fight loneliness, and sometimes I get nervous at night living alone by myself." She said that watching friends get married and having kids can seem to distance friendships. "Suddenly the things we had in common faded as their lives changed," she shared. Lindsey said, "Change is simply a part of life, though, and I believe that people who hold a special place in our hearts will always be there in some capacity, even after we move to a different phase."

The *Catechism* states:

> We must also remember the great number of single persons who, because of the particular circumstances in which they have to live—often not of their choosing—are especially close to Jesus' heart and therefore deserve the special affection and active solicitude of the Church, especially of pastors. Many remain without a human family often due to conditions of poverty. Some live their situation in the spirit of the Beatitudes, serving God and neighbor in exemplary fashion. The doors of

homes, the "domestic churches," and of the great family
which is the Church must be open to all of them. "No
one is without a family in this world: the Church is a
home and family for everyone, especially those who
'labor and are heavy laden.'" (*CCC* 1658).

Our Church calls us to be mindful of the single people
and to open our own domestic churches to them. Visits or
dinners with our single friends, parishioners, and neighbors
give everyone a sense of family vital to us all.

Some single women have wanted to marry, but it just
never worked out for one reason or another. Pope Pius XII
spoke about the single woman and her resignation to God,
even if a little reticently:

> This vocation, this call of love, makes itself felt in very
> diverse manners. . . . But also the young Christian
> woman, remaining unmarried in spite of herself, who
> nevertheless trusts in the providence of the heavenly
> Father, recognizes in the vicissitudes of life the voice
> of the Master: "*Magister adest et vocat te*" (Jn 11:28); It
> is the master, and he is calling you! She responds, she
> renounces the beloved dream of her adolescence and
> her youth: to have a faithful companion in life, to form
> a family! And in the impossibility of marriage she recog-
> nizes her vocation; then, with a broken but submissive
> heart, she also gives her whole self to more noble and
> diverse good works.[1]

One time when I was enjoying a very lovely meal with
my friend Joan Lewis, EWTN's Rome bureau chief in her
dining room in Rome, Italy, we chatted about our families,
and Joan told me, "I did not choose to give up family for a
career. I wanted a happy marriage and family like my parents had, like my myriads of aunts and uncles and, later, my

many cousins had. The Lord, however, had other plans, even though it took me a while to realize they were his!"

Marriage and family just didn't pan out for Joan as she thought it would. But she said, "God, in his wisdom, gave me a very large and very beautiful and very extended family." Joan has scores of nieces, nephews, and great nieces and nephews as well as an extended family that I will tell you about.

Her life is so full and rich. She said,

> I have friends and know families throughout the world, so many of whom are my "second families." I am very close to the North American College, the US seminary in Rome, close to its rectors, to the priests and nuns on its faculty and I follow the path to the priesthood of so many terrific young men—another "family" for me. I have been active in the Santa Susanna parish for decades—close friends, great families. The Paulist priests are yet another "family."

Joan is no slacker. She loves her dynamic life and is faithful to her responsibilities. She told me, "I have a thousand daily responsibilities in my single life and, though my life does not revolve around a husband and children, it is an extremely busy one." But even so, Joan carves out time for her parish family and other worthwhile commitments.

> I make time for one of my favorite things on earth—inviting guests for dinner, bringing people together at table for a good meal, serious conversation and a lot of fun as well. I take time to travel, to attend various board meetings in the States, to cover stories for EWTN, to take time for vacation, and thus to visit my "family" throughout the world.

I was blessed to be one of those people Joan invited to her table. We conversed over dinner and later over a Limoncello that Joan poured for me in a very frosty, cold, elegant glass. I was very much aware of being so close to the heart of the Church—the dome of St. Peter's Basilica (I could just about "touch" it) looked over my shoulder and overshadowed me through Joan's dining room window. The nighttime lights illuminating the massive dome lent a certain mystical aura to our evening. I leaned in and fixated on my friend Joan's words.

This setting was commonplace for Joan every day and evening since her home is situated right near the Vatican to do her reporting, so she can't help but see St. Peter's watching over her. Even though living right in the heart of Rome had become so natural to Joan, she said she never tired of gazing at St. Peter's dome each evening before she retired for the night.

That night during the intimate setting of our dinner together, Joan humbly expressed that if she wasn't a single woman she wouldn't be able to carry out the charity work she does, nor could she interview and entertain so many people at her home or do the traveling she engages in regularly. I was sitting at the same table where many bishops, lay people, priests, and cardinals have sat and enjoyed Joan's friendship and feasts. A number of ambassadors accredited to the Holy See have also graced Joan's table over the years. Joan said, "I am honored to have as friends a number of cardinals and bishops of the Roman Curia and scores of priests, as well as those who are residential prelates."

I should mention that Joan shared all of this with me with the utmost humility. There's no boasting with Joan. Because Joan accepted her call to the single vocation, she has been all over the world covering news events for the Church. When Joan worked as a member of the Holy See delegations to the United Nations conferences, with a Holy See diplomatic passport tucked in her bag, she covered the Cairo Population Conference, the Copenhagen Social Summit, the Beijing Conference on Women, the Istanbul Habitat Conference on Human Settlements, and later two conferences in Doha, Qatar.

Blessed John Paul II had become a focal point of Joan's life. She was with him on fifteen different occasions. Joan's job at the Vatican Information Service (VIS) allowed her the opportunity to read everything the Pope wrote. She said, because of it, "I learned a great deal, and my faith grew as a result."

Joan counted as a friend Monsignor (now Cardinal) Stanislaw Dziwisz. She often brought chocolate chip cookies to him for Blessed John Paul II and the papal household. She said, "Mothers bake cookies for their families, so why couldn't I make them for my Church 'family'?" Covering Blessed John Paul II's beatification "was unparalleled," she said.

And yes, Joan has rubbed elbows with another Pope, too. She's met Pope Benedict XVI on about five different occasions and briefly exchanged a few words with him, usually in his library at the end of a meeting with a visiting head of state or government. "On those occasions I was one of two journalists in a press pool from the Holy See Press Office to cover the visit," she said.

If you won't be sitting in Joan's dining room conversing with her about the Church and life, I'll bet you'll be able to feel her love of life and the Church and learn so much at her blog *Joan's Rome* and at her spots by the same name on EWTN television.[2]

THE VOCATION TO RELIGIOUS LIFE

Another vocation for Catholic women is consecrated religious life. Some consecrated religious women "hear" a distinct calling to religious life. For instance, Blessed Teresa of Calcutta, whom I was so blessed to know, heard a calling from God to become a nun when she was a young girl. It got stronger when she was older, and she became a nun at the age of eighteen because she deeply desired to serve our Lord with her life. Unexpectedly, Mother Teresa heard a second call, too. She has referred to it as her "call within a call." On September 10, 1946, when Sister Teresa was en route to her annual retreat, she heard Jesus distinctly tell her that she was to take care of the "poorest of the poor" beginning in the slums of Calcutta, India. Because of Mother Teresa's yes to God, not once, but twice, through God's grace she has changed the way the world views the poor. She taught us that there is an even greater hunger than the one for food— the one in the human heart. She said the Western world is starved for love in many ways.

St. Teresa of Avila, a Doctor of the Church, had a whole different story when consenting to become a nun and serve God in that vocation. She said she pretty much had to force her own will in order to embrace a religious vocation that did not come easy to her at all. She said, "Though I did not succeed to incline my will to being a nun, I saw that this was the best and safest state, and so, little by little, I determined to force myself to embrace it." She wanted to serve God even though she didn't actually feel an inclination to become a nun or "hear" any sort of call. She said, "When I took the habit, the Lord soon made me understand how greatly he favors those who use force with themselves in serving him."[3]

Earlier in this chapter I referred to Proverbs: "The wise woman builds her house" (Prv 14:1). If you read the next line of that passage, you'll see it says, "But the foolish tears it down with her own hands." Quite honestly, I would need to write a whole book on the ways in which we women do that. But suffice it to say that, if we are wise women, we will build our houses with love and prayer. And if we are not praying and striving to follow God's holy will in our lives, we will inadvertently be tearing down our own houses and families because of our poor choices and the example we will be setting for our families. God is counting on us. He is the one who has placed us in the hearts of our homes to work out our salvations and help those who are near us— our family, our friends, our fellow nuns, our coworkers, and our neighbors—to work out their salvation, too.

A MOMENT TO REFLECT

Women are the hearts of the home. God gives them special nurturing gifts to help all around them. The way we choose to live our lives speaks volumes to not only those who are nearby but also the community and the world. We have the ability to build up or tear down. If we pray, we can do so much good with God's grace.

My Mind to Know Him

1. Have you ever given some thought to how you are "building" your home in whatever state of life you are in? No matter how old we are, we are still working on it!

2. Do you ponder the fact that God calls you to holiness right in the heart of your home, wherever that might be? Take some time to think about what that means to you.

3. Ponder ways you can become more organized in your home. Can you declutter and donate to a local thrift shop or the needy?

My Heart to Love Him

1. Do you consider the events of your life as a road map to holiness? Do you surrender in love to God even in the challenges?

2. Think about your responsibilities in your state in life. Do you approach them with joy and carry them out with love?

3. How do you love God in your home life? Can you list three ways?

My Hands to Serve Him

1. What ways might you make dinnertime in your home more inviting? Can you list three when you have time?

2. Will you keep an eye on the schedules of the people in your home (or extended family if you live alone) and help with making dinnertime a celebration of family?

3. Are you able in your state of life to lend a hand or an ear to someone in need on Sundays?

Seeking God

Dear Lord, show me how to build my house the way that will please you. Fill it with your love. "Protect us, Lord, as we stay awake; watch over us as we sleep, that awake, we may keep watch with Christ, and asleep, rest in his peace" (Canticle of Simeon). Amen.

6. *I*N MY WORK

> You know well enough that our Lord does
> not look so much at the greatness of our
> actions, nor even at their difficulty, but at
> the love with which we do them.
>
> —St. Thérèse of Lisieux

Our places and types of employment furnish us with not
only a paycheck but also many interesting experiences and
many opportunities to minister to the people with whom
we come in contact. Some of my early experiences in the
work force included employment as a grocery clerk, a bak-
ery clerk, a cashier, a waitress, a sous-chef at a French pastry
shop, a private live-in chef and housekeeper, a bartender at
a high-end restaurant, and even a security guard.

When I married and became pregnant with my first
child, I decided to be a stay-at-home mom. I was totally
overjoyed to be a central part of my children's lives and
also to learn along with them on our blessed family journey. This I did for many years. Our family lived with less
of the material comforts in order to be together. At various
times while being home with the kids, I operated a licensed
day-care business and founded and conducted a preschool
program. I also worked as a substitute paraeducator in my

children's schools. I thoroughly enjoyed these roles. I also opened and ran a Catholic book and religious articles store named St. Joseph's Corner. Customers came from all corners of Connecticut and parts of New York to shop there. I wrote and distributed a free newsletter as well.

One particular job that stands out in my mind was working as a life skills instructor at an institute that provided rehabilitation and simple jobs for mentally and physically handicapped adults. I don't think I'll ever forget the clients there. Some areas of the workplace were very intense—truly never a dull moment ever.

On my very first day on the job, I was involved with aiding adults having grand-mal epileptic seizures right in front of me! I also had to skillfully operate a human crane so that I could change diapers on severely handicapped adults. Some clients were dangerous. It was a bit risky caring for them because one never knew if they would go into a psychotic episode or squeeze you too hard. Some also had contagious diseases to boot.

One wheelchair-bound man in his early twenties was always so happy to see me and loved to grab onto my arm whenever I approached—sometimes obsessed with my watch, he pulled me way too hard to draw me nearer. He was merely trying to be friendly, but a couple of times when he could hardly contain his excitement I felt that he could have snapped my arm off because of his brute strength! I learned to keep at arm's length (no pun intended!) from him.

One man brought tears to my eyes the first time I saw him working. His job was to stuff envelopes. He sat in his wheelchair at his station, always smiling. He held up each envelope, one by one, and attempted to put the letter inside while his hands shook uncontrollably. My heart ached watching him concentrate awfully hard and take so long to carry out a very simple act. Yet, he was happy. He was accomplishing something and seemed very proud of his work.

One day I got caught in a very tight spot in between a toilet and a psychotic and physically handicapped woman's motorized wheelchair. I was trying to help the distraught woman who began screaming hysterically because she thought she was stuck. I ended up moving her extremely heavy chair by hand to free her foot since the chair wasn't operating properly. In the process, the entire left side of my body got wrenched and I was in excruciating pain. I later received physical therapy, but because of the injury I was unable to go back to work there.

Looking back, I hope that I brought something special into the lives of these people while I was employed there. That is my hope for whatever job I am involved in.

My godmother, Aunt Bertha, shared a sweet paradox in her life with me. Although a devout Catholic who sings in the choir as a cantor, she once worked as a secretary for a Jewish synagogue. She said she sometimes found herself chuckling inside because of the irony of the situation. I have no doubt though that Aunt Bertha circulated a good measure of Christianity into her workplace! Her smile and the twinkle in her eyes are known to light up a room. Jesus living in her heart was surely radiating throughout the Jewish atmosphere. God has a beautiful sense of humor!

BALANCING OUR TIME

How do we balance our time within the workplace, home life, and the community? I believe a good gauge is to step back and take a look at the whole situation. It's a good idea to ask a few questions. Are you worn out or stressed? Could you be burning the candle at both ends? Perhaps you're doing too much. Do you need to be more aware of getting the proper amount of rest and sleep? You can refer to chapter 2 in which we discuss some of the basic needs we have to care for so we can function as healthy and complete women.

Naturally, we all have those extra busy times in our lives when no matter how much sleep we get or planning we do, there are still numerous demands placed upon us. It could be a tiny baby keeping us up all hours of the night or older children for whom we wait to return safely from being out of the house at night. Crazy hours of employment or care for elderly family members take their toll as well. But when we can have something to say about the schedules in our lives, it's wise to consider how all of our running around or late hours affect our productivity, mood, and even our health.

The fact that we women like to help out can many times stretch us a little too much. It's tough to say no even when we are hesitant to get involved with a project or partici-pate on a committee. Women's hearts are compassionate— that's a fact I don't think anyone can deny. In addition, some might feel guilty if they don't help out. So, try to really think through the invitations you receive to help at school, work, your parish, and in the community. If you're able to help and feel prayerfully called to it—go ahead! If you're reluc-tant, ponder it. If it's imprudent to get involved, graciously bow out. Women need to stop worrying about what others think of them. We shouldn't pile extra stress upon ourselves including pangs of guilt. Instead, let's pray about it and weigh everything out.

A mother e-mailed me and asked for my advice and prayers about her dilemma. She said she really wanted to stay home and raise her children, but she had taken on a part-time job at her children's Catholic school. It was becom-ing more involved than she had expected. The added income wasn't necessary, and she was missing being home with her young two-year-old whom she left with a babysitter. Her husband supported her desire to go back to being a stay-at-home mom. The only reason she felt she couldn't quit her job was that she had become a carpooler for some of the other families and didn't want to disappoint them if she could no longer be a driver.

This poor woman was beating herself up with guilt and felt caught in a quandary. She said, "Please pray that I can overcome worrying about people judging me for my decisions. I care way too much about what others think." She needed me to give her permission to do what her heart was telling her to do. And I did. She was extremely grateful and very relieved. I also suggested that she escape to Jesus in the Blessed Sacrament, pour her heart out to him there, and ask for his peace and guidance. This woman firmed up her decision to leave her part-time job to again be more attentive at home with her family. She told me she is very relieved and extremely happy.

Working mothers often feel looming pressures and strains in juggling their family and their career. Along with the busy schedule and fatigue they experience is often the added feeling of guilt or concern for not being at home as much as they might like to be.

It can sometimes be daunting and even a bit tricky, but we can discover a way to achieve a healthy balance with our work and home schedules and various commitments when we make a point to assess and reassess our routines and situations as well as the people we serve.

INFUSING VIRTUES IN THE WORKPLACE

Living virtuous lives in the workplace at times means reaching out beyond the normal comfort zone. St. Josemaria Escrivá has said, "Each day you must behave towards those around you with genuine understanding, with great affection, together, of course, with all the energy this will call for. Otherwise understanding and affection become complicity and selfishness."[1] We might ask ourselves whether or not we endeavor to reach out to those who are near to us in the workplace and community. Do we just go through the motions of our work, perhaps oblivious to others' needs because we are preoccupied with our own busy thoughts and the task at hand?

When controversy and bullying rears its ugly head in the workplace, it's even harder to exercise the virtues toward the people causing problems. But we must be a Christian example—always.

St. Francis de Sales has said, "It is to those who have the most need of us that we ought to show our love more especially." Sometimes the people with the most need are obvious to us, like the people I mentioned who were physically and mentally handicapped, and we are able to minister to them in some way. Other times, those in need are not so noticeable; our neighbors or coworkers might possess deep hidden wounds and have learned to hide their pain so they can carry on.

But because we pray to radiate Jesus' love to others, we can reach out in friendship to those around us who feel a need to share or seek our advice. Our hope is that, because of our prayerful desire to reach out in some way, the needy might be drawn to the radiance of our Christianity.

Another situation in which a "need" does not seem so apparent is when someone in the workplace is mean or combative in some way. Our Christianity might be mocked at times. And there can be various contradictions and differences of opinion to deal with. It's not so easy to recognize the need of the bully. Yet, he or she might very well be the person to whom our Lord is counting on us to minister. And, yes, it means God wants us to be countercultural. We can do so by praying for them and showing love to them. Love and prayer are powerful!

When I was working as a preschool teacher I was approached by one of the mothers. She asked if we could get together to talk some time, but then she proceeded to just spill it all out right there and then. She was frightened and sensed she could trust me to help. She had recently discovered that she was pregnant and was intensely worried about how she would carry on in her lifestyle and also be able to care for her daughter when her husband wasn't very supportive. We talked quietly awhile right there at the doorway to my classroom, and she knew then that she could come to me for additional advice and encouragement if she needed to. That was almost ten years ago, and to this day we remain friends.

If we want to be a virtuous presence in the workplace and community, getting ensnared in nasty gossip is definitely not a good idea. Women can partake in this sinful pastime, and, yes, men can and do so, too. Sad to say, some people take delight in other's misfortunes or, perhaps even worse, feel the need to start rumors due to jealousy and envy. Certain people are much too curious about other people's business and continuously get entwined in their "investigative work"; spreading rumors is a harmful habit that can ruin someone's reputation and harden our own hearts in the process.

In his book *Consoling the Heart of Jesus: Prayer Companion*, Father Michael Gaitley, M.I.C., said, "Gossip and envy are especially effective at hardening hearts because of the way they twist our emotional responses to the suffering of others." He explained that the twisted emotional perversion might not be immediate, but these sins always steer us that way. He said, when we are of this mindset, "Instead of feeling sorry for someone who suffers, gossip and envy get us to rejoice and delight over his suffering."[2]

A parent I know witnessed some women gossiping in a religious education office while she was helping out there, and because of it she decided to leave the Church. She was appalled that the women in charge of running a Catholic faith formation program were talking behind some of the parishioners' backs. The woman I know didn't merely leave the parish to find a more favorable place to worship; she left the whole Church! Of course, this woman might have had other issues she was dealing with. We don't know. But what we do know is that we must be cognizant of our example— always. Perhaps we could live by the old adage we heard as children, "If you don't have something nice to say, don't say anything at all." It actually boils down to using good manners and common courtesy at all times. Living a prayerful virtuous life will help us to remain on the straight and narrow path that leads to heaven.

Some women might find that they fall into the "Pharisee" category. They lean in towards you and whisper, "Oh, we better pray for Ruth because, you know, she *blah, blah, blah. . . .*" (Fill in the blank with the gossip told in a "Christian" way.) We must watch our tongues! If there is a temptation to speak about someone in a manner that is not charitable, pause and pray. Ask God to help you overcome the temptation. Think before you speak.

I think that we women can become our own worst enemy by worrying that we're not doing enough to please others and God too. We actually heap more responsibilities (whether they be actual or emotional) than is necessary upon our own shoulders. We deal with so many demands for perfection in our lives. Many of the saints spoke about how a whole lot of us might never do very big things in life (or what some might consider "big" things). But we can lead simple yet faithful lives by doing small things with great love. This is very pleasing to God and is actually the secret to real holiness as both St. Thérèse of Lisieux and Blessed Teresa of Calcutta preached. And, yes, God calls all of us to become saints.

Perhaps the irony is that, as many women struggle with the demands of our society and the mass media to become "perfect," achieving perfection is simply being faithful to the duties of our lives. God looks at perfection much differently than do we.

St. Dominic Savio, a student of St. John Bosco, died at the age of fourteen but practiced the heroic virtues in his short life. Understanding the value in offering all of his actions to God, and acknowledging his abilities (or lack thereof), young Dominic said, "I am not capable of doing big things, but I want to do everything, even the smallest things, for the greater glory of God." This is the precise, brilliant attitude for which we should pull out all the stops. The peace of mind that comes with this realization can be life transforming.

What a wonderful feeling it is when we grasp that our Lord simply asks for our faithfulness and not that we build grand cathedrals or have great successes. We don't have to feel overwhelmed. In those tiny yet faithful and prayerful details of our everyday lives lies the secret to deep and eternal happiness.

In my work now, as an author, speaker, and television host, I am in touch with scores of people from around the world who connect with me through my website, blogs, Facebook, letters, and e-mail. I receive so many beautiful letters and e-mails, especially from women who want to tell me how their lives have been impacted by my books or talks and also to express their desire for my prayers and advice. I've often heard from men, too, and even prisoners.

One time I received an e-mail with the words "Get Real" in the subject line. The woman had seen my EWTN show *Everyday Blessings for Catholic Moms* and wanted to warn me, she said, that when my kids got older I would be in a heap of trouble and would then get off my soapbox of encouraging prayer and loving our families in our domestic churches. Perhaps to her I seemed deluded, not knowing the "real" story about kids and problems since my children were still very young. This woman might have meant well; I don't know. The tone of her e-mail was abrasive and her words accusatory; she seemed to have all the answers (to which I would be enlightened as I became a more seasoned mother). She seemed also to imply I was much too positive in my approach.

I wrote a charitable e-mail in return explaining that the small children she sees in the opening of my show were not mine. They were "borrowed" from one of the producers to help create the home-life setting used to enhance the idea of family. I explained to her that I had five children on earth and three in heaven and that my youngest is in college and my oldest is married. I told her that I felt I should put messages out through my show that were full of hope and joy, despite the challenges that come with the vocation of motherhood. She wrote right back to me apologizing for her rash assumptions. I wasn't looking for an apology when I wrote to her, but it was nice to receive it.

Being in the public eye does subject one to criticism, but I am extremely happy that most of the feedback I receive is incredibly positive and affirming. Some messages bring tears to my eyes as women share with me how their lives have been totally transformed by God's amazing grace when they have read my books, watched my show, or heard my talks. I am forever grateful that God would allow me to be a vessel of hope and grace to others through the ministry to women and families that unfolded in my life when I began writing.

Yet, even though my books, articles, shows, and appearances have made it all around the world, it's imperative to remember that all of it began with "tiny details" of being obedient to God's calling in my life—pushing myself to do his holy will even when I am weary or would perhaps rather engage in another activity at that moment. I know I must be faithful and dedicated to doing the work well and getting it completed to the best of my ability and on time (or early), trusting in God's divine providence to work the miracles through it. That, of course, is what he asks of you as well.

A MOMENT TO REFLECT

God works through all of us in all of our walks of life. But he wants us to give him our full permission to operate—the full surrender of our minds, hearts, and souls to him. Wherever we are, no matter what the job, we can radiate God's love.

My Mind to Know Him

1. Do you ever think about evangelizing in the workplace? Will you take some time to ponder how God might be calling you to minister to those who work with you or with whom you serve in some way?

2. Have you prayed about your job and asked God to guide you in your decisions regarding it?

3. Can you think about the balance (or imbalance) of events and activities in your life? If you are a mother of young children and are employed outside the home, can you ponder how you can adapt the schedule to be present to your children as often as possible?

My Heart to Love Him

1. Do you inadvertently turn God off in the workplace? Do you separate your faith life from your work life?

2. How can you infuse virtues into the workplace through praying for an ever-greater attentiveness of others' needs?

3. When praying in the coming days, will you try to surrender your heart more fully to God's holy will in your life? If at all possible, try to spend some time with Jesus in the Blessed Sacrament.

My Hands to Serve Him

1. When you are going about your work this week (at home or outside), try to imagine that Jesus is the one you are serving when you serve others. Ask God to help you.

2. Bearing in mind you don't want to overdo, could there possibly be someone whom our Lord wants you to reach out to in a special helpful way?

3. Ponder a few ways that you can infuse Christian virtues into the workplace in a tangible way. Jot them down and try to carry them out soon.

Seeking God

Dear Lord Jesus, thank you for the workplace in which you have placed me at this point in my life. Help me to be open to the whispers of the Holy Spirit guiding my mind, heart, and hands to serve you in all who surround me. Amen.

7. In My Struggles

Very truly, I tell you, you will weep and
mourn, but the world will rejoice; you will
have pain, but your pain will turn into joy.

—John 16:20

We all know there's absolutely no lack of troublesome things
that can happen to women. And there is a whole host of
challenging issues that women must face. The list includes
sickness, grief, stress, sense of failure, discouragement,
anger, resentment, jealousy, divorce, difficult pregnancies,
loss of a child or spouse, being stretched to the limit, dealing with demands for perfection, and being bombarded
with lopsided messages from the culture. Many women are
exhausted, depressed, and trying to do too much. As we all
know, there really are so many challenges women face.

As we explore these challenges, let's remember that
prayer is always our best first step in facing them. You can
refer back to chapter 4 on prayer as you strive to become
a more prayerful woman to cope with and overcome the
struggles in your life, with God's amazing grace, of course.
Hopefully, throughout this chapter you'll find some Catholic
"tools" to help you handle and address the tough issues

so that, rather than giving into passions and weaknesses at difficult times, you can turn to prayer and hope instead.

STRUGGLES AND VIRTUES

I'll never forget the day the doorbell rang while I was peacefully lying on my couch abiding by my doctor's strict orders for complete bed rest during a very precarious pregnancy. The nurse that was with me at the time answered the door while my children huddled around me, drawing and looking at picture books. The uninvited guest who came through the door was escorted down the hallway by the nurse. As she approached, she formally stretched out her hand to present me a business card. She said, "My name is 'so-in-so' and I am here to investigate child abuse." She didn't bat an eye. The words just rolled off her tongue as plain as someone would say, "Can I borrow a cup of sugar." I was floored. I was shocked, to say the very least. She must have the wrong house. Child abuse? What? I couldn't fathom it. Was this for real? Good thing I was lying down!

Perhaps you can imagine what might have been going through my head. I was a mother with a whole lot of love in my heart and who took my motherhood utterly seriously. I viewed it as a holy vocation in which my husband and I would raise our little saints to heaven. The woman proceeded to tell me that the principals and teachers at my children's schools would be questioned and there would be a concentrated questioning process involving my husband, my children, and me. It would be a long and thorough investigation.

I just couldn't take it. I was not going to allow some stranger to just walk through the front door of my domestic church and inflict all of that craziness on us—causing me to feel falsely accused without having a chance to defend myself. "Mrs. so-in-so, are you finished? Please leave my home; you are upsetting my children. We will call you." So, she left, thank God.

We dealt with the investigation together as soon as my husband was with me to sort it all out. I wanted to shield my children from it as best I could. But, in reality, it affected everyone. Everyone was questioned. We were considered guilty until proven innocent. I wondered who reported suspected child abuse? How long can this go on? We prayed our way through it.

At that time, my rambunctious daughter, Jessica, had a bit of a shiner on one eye. A little jitterbug in her chair, she had slid off and bumped her brow bone on the solid oak leg of our kitchen table one evening. So, we surmised that someone must have seen Jessica's bruised brow and called the authorities, suspecting child abuse. Thankfully, I remembered that right after the table leg incident Jessica was in a shoe store at the local mall and had tripped over a shoe rest. The salesperson brought over some ice in a plastic bag, which was placed on Jessica's sore and swollen face. Of course, I felt sorry for her, but I was happy that the injury had happened in public and that there was a witness. I contacted the store, and the salesperson was able to testify to the authorities that the incident had indeed occurred and was completely innocent. Thank God! All of the teachers and principals gave glowing reports, and the case was eventually dropped. But what a painful ordeal!

In a mother's life many struggles will come to visit. Sometimes they are the demands of parenthood itself—of truly giving of yourself, making the necessary sacrifices for your family. Faithful mothers put their own desires and comforts on hold for the sake of their children. No one ever said it would be easy. In fact, Jesus told us that we are to pick up our cross and follow him. That's sacrificial love, the love that reaches up from a generous mother's heart.

At times, the struggle comes when our children suffer with illness, whether physical, emotional, or psychological. We have to deal with our own sicknesses or fatigue, too. A spouse who is inattentive or not so prayerful can cause us to feel alone in our parenting. At those times, we can reach out more intensely in prayer, asking our Lord for help.

As women we also face rejection. I vividly remember when I was very pregnant with my firstborn. I was so totally happy, thrilled beyond measure, and filled with the intense joy of a young expectant mother. My bubble of joy burst quickly when it was pierced by a huge thorn of rejection. My heart, in fact, felt pummeled when my husband and I were turned away from a house rental. It would have been the perfect little home for our new family. We had begun our search for a home of our own after leaving our live-in positions as cook and housekeeper for a family in Connecticut.

My visibly showing unborn baby must have seemed like the plague to the woman who rejected us. Children were uncompromisingly not allowed in her rental bungalow we learned. I felt so totally rejected and a bit hopeless too as a young mother wanting desperately to start "feathering a nest" that we could call home. For one reason or another, we faced continuous rejection in our pursuit.

Looking back, I think of Mary and Joseph feeling the sting of rejection as they were turned away just as they were about to welcome their newborn king in childbirth. With God's grace and providence, their story ended as perfectly as it was meant to. It did for us, too. After much patience, prayer, and perseverance, we settled into our new home before our son Justin was born.

When my mother was dying of cancer, I would visit her in the hospital. One night, as I was about to go home, I leaned over to hug and kiss her. I held my eighteen-month-old daughter Chaldea close to my mother so she could kiss her good night. My mother unexpectedly said, "I won't be here to watch her grow up." My heart broke right then.

Another profound loss occurred when I was sixteen weeks' pregnant with one of my babies. When I started to cramp with contractions and bleeding I went to the doctor and was given an ultrasound. It revealed a sixteen-week-old baby without a heartbeat. Since I was so far along the doctor told me I would need a D and C with suction. I shuddered. That would be an abortion if my baby were alive. I couldn't take that chance. Maybe the ultrasound was wrong. Maybe the technician couldn't see the heartbeat. I asked if I could go home to rest and wait.

At home, the contractions continued, and all night long I passed clots of blood. The pain was unbearable. I went to the hospital in the morning for another ultrasound—still, no heartbeat. I cried. My doctor told me I had to be wheeled into surgery right away. I was moved by the tears that came down my pro-life doctor's face. He united his heart to mine.

I woke up from my surgery in another room with a nurse telling me that I had lost a lot of blood and would be staying overnight. I had a couple of IVs in my arms and was getting a blood transfusion. I told her that my children wouldn't understand, and I needed to go home. She told me I simply could not. I pleaded with my doctor when he came to my room to check on me. I promised to stay in bed and have my family care for me. He smiled and knew he would have trouble arguing with me and so let me go home.

It wasn't until the next day that I learned the whole story. My caring doctor called to check on me, and after we went over a few things, I asked him why it hurt every time I took a breath. He then told me what happened. "As soon as you went under the anesthesia, you hemorrhaged profusely. You lost so much blood that your blood pressure plummeted to almost nothing and we had to save your life. The pain you feel in your throat when you breathe is from the breathing tube we inserted down your throat. If that hemorrhage had happened anywhere but that operating room, you would have died for sure." Wow. Thank you, dear Jesus.

Years later, I pondered the whole scenario, and it was then that it really hit me that I was so close to death. But I wouldn't have had it any other way. I needed to wait and be absolutely sure that my baby had died before I had that surgery.

At times, certain events of our lives can be overwhelming. We might be enduring heartache or pain, dealing with illness, or feeling confused or scared and not really knowing what to do. I think it can be a great comfort to take to heart that our Lord knows what is good for us at every moment, even when it doesn't seem so. Excuse me, I should say, our Lord knows what is *perfect* for us!

If it seems like I am suggesting God is a masochist, happily inflicting pain, heartache, and serious illnesses upon us, please bear with me. That is not at all what I want to say. I only mean that God knows us through and through, and as the Divine Physician, he allows us to live through certain situations to bring us closer to him in our prayers. God permits suffering in our lives because He knows a greater good will come from it.

If we are honest, we would realize, if we had everything our own way, like spoiled children, we might end up in hell (not that hell is what we were hoping for!). Our choices might not be conducive to the spiritual journey God knows is absolutely necessary for our eternal salvation.

The allurements of the world can indeed cloud our eternal vision. Therefore, we should pray to live the life God wants for us.

Jesuit Jean-Pierre de Caussade (1675–1751) said,

> What God arranges for us to experience at each moment is the best and holiest thing that could happen to us. ... Every moment we live through is like an ambassador who declares the will of God, and our hearts always utter their acceptance. We can find all that is necessary in the present moment. ... At every moment God's will produces what is needed for the task at hand, and the simple soul, instructed by faith, finds everything as it should be and wants neither more nor less than what it has.[1]

Let's explore this concept and how we might strive to become that "simple soul."

It's no secret that women experience deep heartache at times. Many years ago I had to seek temporary financial assistance and food stamps from the welfare department due to reasons beyond my control. I was soon to give birth to my third living child (I then had two living children and had lost three to miscarriages). It would be another Cesarean section. Without warning, my husband suddenly left me. It was a very painful and shocking breakup.

While traveling to an out-of-town location, my husband unexpectedly pulled the car over to the side of the road, opened the driver's door, and got out. "I'm leaving," he simply stated and he started walking. He stuck his thumb out to hitchhike and got into the first car that pulled over. Just like that, he abandoned us. I sat there paralyzed in the passenger seat. I was aware that things had not been perfectly harmonious between us, but I was hoping and praying we could work it out somehow. Sitting there, I had to face the facts rather quickly. I was now alone, in the car on the side of the road, with my young daughter. She began to sob uncontrollably after witnessing every bit of the insanity that had just occurred.

Her cries snapped me out of my momentary paralysis, and I clambered into the backseat to comfort her. After a few minutes, I had to get behind the wheel and start driving. I wondered how I would break the news to my son when he got home from school later that afternoon. Thinking back on that conversation with him still brings a stinging pain to my heart.

A few months later, now a single mother of three, there was a knock at my front door. It was a representative from the welfare department showing up to do a surprise inspection on my apartment. She told me that they suspected I was living with a man and if that were true they would terminate my benefits immediately.

I wanted to scream. *Why should I be violated like this just because they suspected something?* The baby was now awake from her rudely interrupted nap, and I was thoroughly flustered. My personal items were about to be rummaged through, and even worse, I was being falsely accused of something I would never do. I simply did not want that stranger in my home!

As the inspector proceeded, I stretched out my hand and passionately pointed to the picture of the Sacred Heart of Jesus hanging on my living room wall and blurted out, "That's the man I live with!" I sincerely hope that my zealous declaration of faith touched her in some way. Thankfully, there were no more surprise inspections after that, and the officials concluded I was abiding completely by all of their rules. And thank God, after a while I no longer required the assistance.

Another kind of suffering or struggle women can experience is illustrated in the story I am about to share. Once when I was leaving the post office, a Catholic man I knew, who was walking through the parking lot, stopped to say hello. He proceeded to tell me that he was now divorced because his wife "just did not yield" to him and that all of their troubles stemmed directly from the fact that his wife would not be subject to him. *That poor woman*, I thought. I confess that at that very moment I did not feel one ounce of pity for that man. My immediate concern was for his ex-wife, precisely because of what he had said.

This idea that wives should be submissive to their husbands is an enormous struggle for many Christian women. They feel intimidated by the words in the Letter to the Ephesians. But their fears arise from a huge misinterpretation of the text. I love how Blessed John Paul II brilliantly unearthed the real meaning in those complex words in *Mulieris Dignitatem*. He impresses upon us the need for "the sincere gift of self" of each spouse:

> The author of the Letter to the Ephesians sees no contradiction between the exhortation formulated in this way and the words: "Wives, be subject to your husbands, as to the Lord. For the husband is the head of the wife" (5:22–23). The author knows that this way of speaking, so profoundly rooted in the customs of the time, is to be understood and carried out in a new way; as a *"mutual subjection out of reverence for Christ"* (cf. Eph 5:21). This is especially true because the husband is called the "head" of the wife *as* Christ is the head of the Church; he is so in order to give "himself up for her" (Eph 5:25), and giving himself up for her means giving up even his own life. However, whereas in the relationship between Christ and the Church the subjection is only on the part of the

Church, in the relationship between husband and wife
the "subjection" is not one-sided but mutual. (*MD* 24)

If you haven't read *Mulieris Dignitatem* (*On the Dignity
and Vocation of Women*), I highly recommend that you do.
Even if you have, it's a good idea to read it over and over
again. It will certainly lift your spirits.

Down through the ages women have been forced to
grapple with cultural issues. What about today's culture?
In many respects the issues today are far more challenging. Women often struggle due to the temptations they feel
to pursue the alluring but false promises of our ungodly
culture. On the other hand, they can feel exhausted from
the strenuous battle to prevent the dangerous and damag-
ing cultural influences from affecting or harming them and
their families.

The false life portrayed on billboards, sung in popular music, watched on reality TV, and transmitted all over
social media can begin to seem real. We can get entangled
in the culture without realizing it or recognizing its dangers.
We see wealth and materialism portrayed as a norm to be
achieved, and we might strive to acquire way too many
things. We can become like zombies to technology, obsessed
with gathering information, so preoccupied with the news
that we totally miss out on the present moment.

We should keep in mind some simple yet poignant
words from St. John Vianney: "You cannot please both God
and the world at the same time. They are utterly opposed to
each other in their thoughts, their desires, and their actions."
If we get serious about our prayer lives and seek out
solid Catholic teaching materials to absorb, listen to, read,
and nurture our faith (I highly recommend EWTN television and radio), we will be greatly aided to keep our eyes
on heaven and its rewards and what we need to be doing

to work out our salvation, instead of chasing after society's allurements and listening to the demands put upon us from an ungodly world.

We read in Romans 6:12, "Therefore, do not let sin exercise dominion in your mortal bodies, to make you obey their passions." Sin can be such a sneaky thing. It can creep up on you and make you very ill in more ways than one. I am reminded of the three times that I have had Lyme disease. It comes from the bite of an itty-bitty tick (an external parasite arachnid) carrying the disease. Through its bite the infection goes in the body and straight away attacks the central nervous system. The tick can be merely the size of a poppy seed. Because I live in the country and in Connecticut where Lyme disease was discovered, I had the misfortune of getting very sick with the disease too many times already. Thankfully, a strong and long dose of an antibiotic helps to alleviate symptoms, but there are varying schools of thought on its complete cure. Some experts believe the disease stays in your system forever.

In any case, I think of the miniscule tick and, if it's carrying the disease, the enormous amount of damage that can be done if one is bitten; if not treated for the proper length of time, the disease could end up killing, same as sin. Sin can start off slight or "tiny" (so we think) but can wreak so much havoc in our lives both spiritually and physically. A guilty conscious can bring on tremendous stress. My friend Father Bill C. Smith used to say that being in sin is like walking around with a huge sack of potatoes on your back. And thank God sin does affect us, so we are motivated to get to Confession. But many have become numb to what their conscience tells them because they enjoy sin too much, and it deceptively eats away at their mind, body, and soul. When we sin, even a little, we damage ourselves big time. There's no such thing as a good sin. Thank God we can go to Confession, be renewed, and start again. We can make a habit of examining our consciences daily. The evening is a good time. We can ask our Lord for forgiveness for our shortcomings (and sins, of course) before we close our eyes to sleep.

Another struggle women may undergo is in being misunderstood at times and that can sometimes make it tough to reach out in charity. Years ago my young children and I befriended an elderly man (in his late eighties) who began attending Mass at our parish. He seemed a bit lost at first, perhaps that's why our hearts went out to him. We pointed him in the direction of the coffee and doughnuts served in our church hall after Mass, poured him a cup and sat down with him to talk. He returned each Sunday for some time and always seemed very pleased to see us. We exchanged phone numbers and I called him from time to time during the week since he said he lived alone. I don't think I was ever so shocked as when he elatedly told me that he had been having dreams about me for which he thought he could be arrested. I realized then that he was attracted to me for perverse reasons and not for the charity my children and I bestowed upon him. It's a shame we women have to deal with this kind of thing when we are attempting to extend ourselves in love to others.

Women are very good at feeling guilty (when they shouldn't be) and feeling a tremendous need to escape, too. I'll get into the escaping part in a minute. But even if we women have nothing to be guilty of—that big, dark cloud of guilt seems to be right there looming over us ready to tap us on the shoulder and snatch us up. Maybe we are conditioned as women to take on the blame of almost everything. It's something we need to stop doing.

I so keenly remember hearing about an acquaintance in her early thirties who had committed suicide. My heart nearly broke as I recalled one of the last things she had said to me when I happened to bump into her out in town at a place she was working. I asked her if she was still teaching, and she said, "Well, Donna, I sort of took another journey." She didn't expound upon that, and she was in her work environment with lots of people around, so we couldn't get into any more.

After I left her that day, I planned to look her up (I never knew her phone number or where she lived) and get in touch to see how she was doing since something sounded amiss in her statement to me that day. But, alas, life took on a life of its own as it can do, and I didn't get in touch. Then I heard the news of her untimely death. Could I have said something that would have helped her? I don't know, but I can't beat myself up with guilt trying to figure that out. Instead, I turn my thoughts to God each and every time she comes to my mind, and believe me, these times were many after finding out about her premature death. And I pray for her soul and for her family.

Women often feel a need to escape, too. Perhaps we can't blame ourselves since we have so much to contend with. Women sometimes run away from something unpleasant or too tough to deal with by grabbing the remote (too much television), the computer mouse (too much Internet and social media), the refrigerator door (overeating), the wine bottle (excessive drinking), prescription drugs, bad associations (ungodly relationships), and so on.

We can also try to escape to forms of isolation. Unless we are called by God to be a hermit, God does not want us to be alone. He tells us in Genesis, "It is not good that the man should be alone" (2:18). St. Francis of Assisi on the way to "lady poverty" knew he couldn't go alone and so had a friend in the journey, St. Clare of Assisi. At those times we most want to isolate ourselves, it might help to speak with a spiritual director or a trusted friend or family member, to air out our fears and concerns. There are many ways to avoid being alone in the spiritual life. In addition to meeting with a spiritual director or someone to talk to about a certain situation, surrounding oneself with like-minded faithful Catholics will immensely help all involved on the spiritual journey. We need to help one another not to feel alone.

God wants us to escape to him—to his Sacred Heart. If we find ourselves wanting to escape something, let's pause and examine it, face it, and try to discern it. Let's make wise choices about how to respond to the situation. Divine help will always renew us in some way, even when we don't feel it.

REDEMPTIVE ASPECTS OF SUFFERING

When baby Jesus was presented in the Temple, Simeon, guided by the Holy Spirit, blessed Jesus, Mary, and Joseph. He told Mary that her child was destined for the rise and fall of many in Israel; he would be a sign that would be opposed, "and a sword will pierce your own soul too" (Lk 2:35).

Blessed John Paul II has said in *Mulieris Dignitatem*, "As we contemplate this Mother, whose heart 'a sword has pierced,' our thoughts go to all the suffering women in the world, suffering either physically or morally." He goes on to explain that, even though women seem to endure suffering better than men, her sensitivity comes into play. He said, "In this suffering a woman's sensitivity plays a role, even though she often succeeds in resisting suffering better than a man" (*MD* 19).

With deep compassion and a thorough understanding, the late pope listed many forms of suffering for women, including the sufferings of mothers, widows, single women, and women who have been exploited. He explained, "It is difficult to enumerate these sufferings; it is difficult to call them all by name" (*MD* 19).

Women suffer from the many invisible wounds, too. Blessed John Paul II said, "Then there are the sufferings of consciences as a result of sin, which has wounded the woman's human or maternal dignity: the wounds of consciences which do not heal easily. With these sufferings too we must place ourselves at the foot of the Cross" (*MD* 19).

And we must certainly follow Blessed John Paul II's advice and place all of our sufferings at Jesus' feet. The *Catechism* teaches:

> It is not easy for man, wounded by sin, to maintain moral balance. Christ's gift of salvation offers us the grace necessary to persevere in the pursuit of the virtues. Everyone should always ask for this grace of light and strength, frequent the sacraments, cooperate with the Holy Spirit, and follow his calls to love what is good and shun what is evil. (*CCC* 1811)

Let's not forget to ask for those imperative graces to lead holy lives.

Regarding our suffering and pain, we must never forget the "end of the story." This is so very important because it is filled with joy that no one can rob from us. Blessed John Paul II points out,

> But the words of the Gospel about the woman who suffers when the time comes for her to give birth to her child, immediately afterwards express *joy*: it is *"the joy that a child is born into the world."* This joy too is referred to the Paschal Mystery, to the joy which is communicated to the Apostles *on the day of Christ's Resurrection*: "So you have sorrow now" (these words were said the day before the Passion); "but I will see you again and

your hearts will rejoice, and no one will take your joy
from you." (Jn 16:22–23; *MD* 19)

Our hearts will rejoice, and no one will take that joy from
us! Certainly, these are profound, life-changing words to
keep tucked away in our hearts.

Earlier, I discussed believing that God knows what is
right for our souls. As Catholics we view suffering differently from most other religions. We recognize a beautiful
redemptive aspect of suffering. When we pray, we endeavor
to unite our prayers to the holy sacrifice of the Mass that
is being celebrated somewhere throughout the world at
every hour of every day. We do this when we participate at
Mass and also through our morning offering: "I offer you
my prayers, works, joys, and suffering of this day in union
with the Holy Sacrifice of the Mass throughout the world."

The Mass is powerful. It is the highest form of prayer.
What Jesus did for us when he hung on the Cross was more
than powerful. Words simply cannot describe it. What he
continues to do for us now during each and every Mass is
powerful, too. The sacrifice of the Mass and the sacrifice
of the Cross are the same; only, the sacrifice of the Cross is
repeated in an unbloody manner at each Mass. Jesus gives
us his Body and Blood—he gives us himself in the Eucharist
just as he did on the Cross. When we unite our prayers and
sufferings to the power of the Mass, miracles happen.

When preaching about the amazing power of the Mass,
Cardinal Raymond Leo Burke (prefect of the Supreme Tri-
bunal of the Apostolic Signatura) said,

> Our Lord Jesus Christ will receive our poor, troubled
> and sinful hearts into his own glorious Sacred Heart,
> through the Eucharistic Sacrifice. He will make our
> hearts rich in love for the service of our brothers and sis-
> ters. Nourished at the altar of Christ's Sacrifice with the

incomparable food of his true Body and Blood, healed and strengthened, may we go forth to bring the love of God to all our brothers and sisters, especially those who hunger to know the truth and to receive the love, which God alone can give them.[2]

If we reflect on St. Paul's words, "I am now rejoicing in my sufferings for your sake, and in my flesh I am completing what is lacking in Christ's afflictions for the sake of his body, that is, the church" (Col 1:24), perhaps we can understand what it means to unite our sufferings to Jesus' sufferings to help save souls. Of course, nothing was "lacking" in Christ's sufferings. We can believe St. Paul meant that the grace and mercy from Jesus' sufferings is not accepted by all and that, when we offer our own sufferings in union with our Lord's, others will be helped.

St. Benedicta of the Cross (Edith Stein) reminded us, "To drink the chalice with the Lord (Mt 20:21) means dying to one's natural self—both in the sensitive and in the spiritual part. Only in this way can one enter the narrow way." As Catholics we are to "enter through the narrow gate; for the gate is wide and the road is easy that leads to destruction, and there are many who take it. For the gate is narrow and the road is hard that leads to life, and there are few who find it" (Mt 7:13–14). Sobering warnings, indeed! Yet they are so full of hope, as well. We must keep our eyes on the narrow gate ahead and keep away from the snares of the world.

In his retreats Father Hardon would always impress upon the attendees that it is absolutely necessary to practice heroic virtue in order to lead a holy life and survive in our world today. He wasn't happy with just plain old virtues. They needed to be *heroic*. He said, if Catholics in the early Church had not been faithful and heroic believers, "nothing

would have happened. The Church would have died out
before the end of the first century."

The *Catechism* tells us:

> A virtue is a habitual and firm disposition to do good.
> It allows the person not only to perform good acts, but
> to give the best of himself. The virtuous person tends
> toward the good with all his sensory and spiritual
> powers; he pursues the good and chooses it in concrete
> actions. (CCC 1803)

Father Hardon warned us, "For Catholic parents to live
good Catholic lives in our day requires heroic virtue. Only
heroic parents will survive the massive, demonic seculariza-
tion of materially super-developed countries like America."[3]
He certainly did not mince words, did he?

And that was around twenty years ago. Since then we
know that our culture has increasingly deteriorated. The
mass media is overflowing with sexual content, for instance,
and portrays violence greater than ever before.

Father Hardon was specific with regard to the types of
heroic virtues we must use and why. He said,

> If we are going to re-evangelize, or for our present pur-
> pose, convert our nation from this self-idolatry which
> has become the religion of our nation, we must live
> utterly, absolutely selfless lives ourselves. Never, in my
> estimation, has the world had more need for saints than
> today. A saint, by the Church's own definition, is one
> who practices heroic virtue. . . . I will choose especially
> four virtues that we must practice, and practice hero-
> ically. We must practice heroic faith, heroic patience,
> heroic chastity, and heroic charity. . . . In today's world,
> and in our own beloved America, we must have the faith
> of martyrs. You cannot get away with anything less.

Father Hardon explained that heroic patience is "the willing endurance of extraordinary suffering. There must be extraordinary suffering, patiently endured, by those who believe in Christ as the God-Man who died on the Cross to redeem the world." He cautioned, "Never run away from the Cross. Never. Because that's how the new paganism came into existence. And the people, millions that call themselves Christians, are pagans, because paganism is Christianity without the Cross. If we are to convert these new pagans, we must practice heroic chastity."[4]

While writing this book I received a phone call from my doctor one evening. He gave me a diagnosis that many women dread. Quite honestly I wasn't one of those women. It never entered my mind as a possibility. I was too busy to think of it and felt I was too healthy and too young to be inflicted with the disease.

"I just got the results from your bone density test," he said. "Your bones are too thin—you have osteoporosis. If you fall you'll fracture your hip or your spine." Then he straight away went on to tell me the available medical treatments and asked which one I wanted him to prescribe. I told him that I was a bit shocked by the news and needed some time to research the disease and the medications. I am not one to blindly take a medication just because it is prescribed to me. I believe that we all need to be our own best advocates, as well as to be an educated patient when it comes to our health. He was okay with that and told me to get back to him when I was ready.

Well, I can't say that I jumped for joy about that phone call. It floored me. The following day I felt depressed and shocked all at once, and maybe a little angry at myself, for not getting the test done sooner and because of the bad car accident I was in over four years ago that prevented me from exercising, which is so important in maintaining bone mass (especially when approaching or going through menopause). I moped around trying to digest it all. *I'm sorry, Lord, for not trusting you more with this. Forgive me for my bad attitude.*

With God's grace and my determination, I snapped out of my funk that very day. I prayed for God's will whatever it would be. After doing my research, which revealed the dangerous side-effects from the medications offered at that time, I decided to take a proactive natural approach and began taking special bone-building supplements. Additionally, I immediately started a regimen of doing at least thirty minutes of weight bearing exercises (known for building bone mass) every morning. I'm determined to get better with God's help. I'll revisit the situation in a year when I undergo another bone density test. Meanwhile, I'll be eating well, taking my supplements, walking, and praying.

That fateful phone call gave me reason to adjust my schedule and resolve. I am thoroughly enjoying my early morning walks out in God's beautiful creation. It's a marvelous time to convene with God, our Blessed Mother, and the saints too, while listening to the birds singing and observing the beauty of nature all around me.

Earlier, I mentioned St. Paul's words "I am now rejoicing in my sufferings for your sake, and in my flesh I am completing what is lacking in Christ's afflictions for the sake of his body, that is, the church" (Col 1:24). Can we jump up for joy about our sufferings? Maybe not? Maybe yes? Maybe a little? Let's at least be sure to offer them all to Jesus with love and pray that souls can be saved.

As we ponder our spiritual lives, we can consider St. Leo the Great's excellent reminder, "Virtue is nothing without the trial of temptation, for there is no conflict without an enemy, no victory without strife." He tells us that, if it were not for those pesky and even terrible sufferings, we wouldn't have the victory of heaven. Let's ask for guidance from the Holy Spirit to show us how to use the heroic virtues in our lives. Let's also remember that we can offer up our sufferings to God and pray for his help, as we discussed in chapter 4 on prayer. Blessed Mother Teresa taught the sick and dying she cared for to offer their sufferings. We must not waste suffering.

Women who are hurting or know others who are hurting pray for relief. In the course of just one day, any number of requests can come in to me through e-mail, Facebook messages, letters, and phone calls, asking for prayers for a myriad of situations; most of them are very serious needs. Women care so much for others and desire in some way to stop pain and suffering. It's what women do.

I think of a mother running to her crying baby to comfort him or hastening to pick up a child who has fallen and scraped her knee. Medicine, a bandage, a kiss, and a hug from a mother makes things right again. The loving mother wants to take pain away from her adult children, too, but there's only so much she is able to do. Through her prayers, she can ask God for the medicine, the bandage, and the healing love of the kiss and hug.

Prayers, as we know, are not always answered in the manner in which we had hoped. Miracles do happen, but not everyone is healed of illness or suffering. Yet, we never stop hoping. When prayer requests come in, I pray right at that moment for relief, for healing, and for God's holy will for that person. I know in my heart and from experience that God's medicine, bandage, and love is delivered in various forms, and we leave that up to the Divine Physician who knows what is absolutely best for each of us.

We should consider that long illnesses, like those most often endured by an elderly person, might be unavoidable. But they can be the medicine needed to soften the heart and

seek God before one passes from this world to the next. For
other people experiencing serious illness or suffering, their
miracle might be in offering their pain and suffering to God,
which he uses to heal someone else's heart and soul. We
leave it all in God's hands.

Sometimes the pain of our struggles seems overwhelming. But we must remember that our Lord is with us always
and has promised us that he will wipe away every tear. My
Aunt Bertha was utterly crushed when her daughter Cathy
died of a massive coronary unexpectedly in her early fif-
ties, just a few months after Aunt Bertha's husband Edward
died. A couple of months after Cathy passed away, I had
mentioned something in an e-mail to Aunt Bertha about
singing for joy, since she is a choir member at her parish.
She answered my e-mail and told me that the only time
she doesn't feel pain or grief is when she sings at church.
Singing eased her pain. Her heart was praying twice, as the
saying goes.

St. Paul tells us, "Present yourselves to God as those
who have been brought from death to life" (Rom 6:13). Let
us endeavor to let go of resentments and offer our hurt to
God. Let's practice the virtues, pray for forgiveness, and
offer forgiveness to others with patient hearts. Let's trust
in God's wisdom, while doing our best to sing for joy and
forge ahead with God's grace to grow in holiness.

A MOMENT TO REFLECT

St. Francis de Sales said, "All the science of the Saints is
included in these two things: To do, and to suffer. And
whoever had done these two things best, has made himself
most saintly."[5] It's so important to remember the amazing
redemptive aspect of suffering and not to waste our suffering and pain. Our Blessed Mother when she appeared

in Fatima, Portugal, asked Lucia, Francesco, and Jacinta to offer sufferings and penances to atone for the sins of others. Be sure to put your sufferings to good use!

As we navigate our rich but challenging lives as Catholic women, let's also do our very best to keep these words of Jesus in our hearts: "So you have pain now; but I will see you again, and your hearts will rejoice, and no one will take your joy from you" (Jn 16:22).

My Mind to Know Him

1. Do you stop to ponder God and his holy will when you are undergoing some sort of struggle? If not, can you endeavor to think of him no matter what is happening in your life?

2. Can you carve out a bit of time to read about the lives of the saints so you will learn about the saints' struggles and virtues?

3. Is there someone in your life to whom you can be an example of grace under fire? List three ways you might inspire him or her.

My Heart to Love Him

1. Is there someone in your life who is suffering? Can you think of a way to offer Christian solace? Can you ask God to help you be more attentive to the needs of others around you?

2. Throughout your struggles, can you offer your heart more fully to God and ask for his graces for you and those you serve?

3. Can you take some time and think of someone who has hurt you? Will you contact that person and offer

forgiveness if you have not already done so? If you cannot contact that person, will you hold that person up in
prayer and ask God to help him or her?

My Hands to Serve Him

1. The next time you are required to do a task you don't
   particularly care for, offer it to God in love (which means
   no complaining) and strive to do it to the best of your
   ability.

2. Can you bake a treat for, make a meal for, or send a
   cheery card to someone who is struggling in some way?

3. Can you take a few minutes sometime in the next few
   days to ponder a "prayer of action"? List a few and then
   try to carry one out soon. It can be something like bringing fresh flowers or a plant to a shut-in and then spending some time with him or her.

Seeking God

Dear Lord, Jesus, thank you for my life! Thank you for constantly
offering me countless opportunities to turn to you in prayer and
to help others in need. Please forgive me for my complaints when
things aren't going along as I would like. Help me to fully trust
you with my life. Amen.

PART FOUR

MEETING CHRIST IN OTHERS

In the same way, let your light shine before others, so that they may see your good works and give glory to your Father in heaven.

—Matthew 5:16

8. A WOMAN FOR OTHERS

Here am I, the servant of the Lord.

—Luke 1:38

The phrase "a woman for others" could actually sum up our lives as Catholic women. We care for the many people with whom God surrounds us—our families and all those near us in every walk of life.

One way we connect with others is by keeping in touch with extended family. Nowadays, families are spread all over and disconnected due to work and other situations. It makes staying connected somewhat challenging. Thankfully, technology such as e-mail and phones make it so much more possible. We can even see one another in real time through video calls.

Perhaps, if you have not been in touch with a relative in some time, you are putting that off because you don't know what to say. But you can just pick up the phone and dial. You'll be glad you did, and your relative will be, too.

We can be women for others in the parish communities by volunteering in some capacity. You might become a lector, a greeter, an extraordinary minister of the Eucharist, or a teacher in the religious education program. We can be women for others in the community, through friendships, by mentoring, and in so many ways. As I mentioned earlier, God does not want us to be alone. We can instinctively reach out and use our God-given womanly gifts to touch others in innumerable of ways.

Our Lord wishes to "send" us as a light to others, an essential light in a darkened world. I'll explain what this means by recalling Blessed John Paul II's words. He said, "Do not be slow to answer the Lord's call! From the passage of the Book of Exodus read to us in this Mass we can learn how the Lord acts in every vocation (cf. Ex 3:1–6, 9–12). First, he provokes a new awareness of his presence—the burning bush. When we begin to show an interest he calls us by name."

I'm sure you are aware of God's presence in your life, and you desire to respond to him in some way. Perhaps that's why you are reading this book. Blessed John Paul II wrote, "When our answer becomes more specific and like Moses we say: 'Here I am' (cf. v. 4), then he reveals more clearly both himself and his compassionate love for his people in need. Gradually he leads us to discover the practical way in which we should serve him: 'I will send you.'"

God will send *me*? But what can I offer? We might wonder. Blessed John Paul II explains, "And usually it is then that fears and doubts come to disturb us and make it more difficult to decide. It is then that we need to hear the Lord's assurance: I am with you (Ex 3:12). Every vocation is a deep personal experience of the truth of these words: 'I am with you'" (homily, January 13, 1995).

As you ponder what these words mean to you personally, let's also look at how the virtues are involved in being a woman for others, sent forth by God in this world. We discussed the virtues in the last chapter on our struggles and our work environment. Remember, virtue is a habitual and firm disposition to do good. We *will* it. We ask God for his grace to receive virtue.

"To Become Like God"

St. Gregory of Nyssa said, "The goal of a virtuous life is to become like God." Perhaps that seems very daunting. But in essence it's really what we strive to do as Catholic women. An important part of the road to holiness is in using the virtues. St. Catherine of Sienna in her *Treatise of Divine Providence* taught that all of the virtues are connected—that if a person possesses one virtue, he or she possesses them all by God's grace. But she believed that God gives each faithful person a particular virtue that is woven through all they do and that this virtue enables the person to grow in all the virtues. While practicing the principal virtue through which divine love shines powerfully, the others will be illuminated and increased.

In his *Introduction to the Devout Life*, St. Francis de Sales talks about the virtues that God gives the saints, and he recommends that each of us should aim for a particular virtue to practice (but not to the exclusion of others). He gives examples of saints who were devoted to certain virtues that became apparent in what they did with their lives. He taught that the value of the virtue is determined by the degree of God's love shining through it. Francis also gave an example of beautiful embroidered flowers and said we should be spiritually "embroidering" throughout our lives using the chief thread of our core virtue.

We must try to envision what our core thread might be or what it could be with prayer. If we aren't aware of a core virtue working in our life, we shouldn't worry, it will come. Our prayers and desire to live a virtuous life will unfold beautifully, and we'll discover our core virtue. As Blessed Mother Teresa would say, "Make your life something beautiful for God." And we can!

St. Francis de Sales said,

> And so some of God's servants devote themselves to nursing the sick, helping the poor, teaching little children in the faith, reclaiming the fallen, building churches, and adorning the altar, making peace among men. In this they resemble embroideresses who work all manner of silks, gold and silver on various grounds, and thus produce beautiful flowers. In the same way the pious souls who undertake some special devout practice use it as the ground of their spiritual embroidery, and frame all kinds of other graces upon it, ordering their actions and affections better by means of this chief thread which runs through all of them.[1]

When I was a teenager, I loved to embroider blue jeans and jean jackets. I wasn't a hippie, although my kids tease me that I must have been since I lived through that era. But I enjoyed creating scenes and pictures on clothing using colorful embroidery floss. I didn't use "all manner of silks, gold and silver," but nonetheless, I fashioned many vibrant images. One I made for a Christian musician was of a golden chalice with a host suspended above it, which graced the back of a jean jacket. I did another of a glorious sunset over a beach to fill another request. I mostly delighted in embroidering flowers and vines and doing natural designs. Those were the days when I had time to sit and embroider! Now, I "embroider" words, among other things.

We women can envision our lives as an exquisite tapestry that we embroider and weave each day. What is your chief "thread"? Perhaps you'll pray and ponder this question.

God Sends Us Forth

So, God sends us forth. He wants us to be a beautiful example of his love to all we meet—the stiff clerk at the post office, the grocery cashier with the tattoos and piercings, the delivery guy, the irritable coworker, the guy who gives you the finger in the grocery store parking lot, and the lonely elderly neighbor—to everyone we naturally come in contact with.

We represent the Church to them. All kinds of conversations can ensue in which our faith is professed when we are out and about. I can tell you so many stories of inspirational conversations that came to pass in the post office. I love when God and our faith is uttered out loud in a government office (which happens a lot when I am around). In addition to the interesting conversations that can occur, the *joie de vivre* of our simple smile or the kind words to someone when we are out doing our errands can be just the medicine needed to help someone through a struggle or pain.

One time when at a department store I mentioned the subject of prayer, regarding my daughter Mary-Catherine studying abroad, to the woman at the checkout counter. It naturally came out in our little exchange when I explained that praying for Mary-Catherine and prayer in general is how I cope with her being so far away for so long. The woman totally understood and told me her faith and prayers kept her sane! This was a very simple exchange in a public place, talking about God—I love weaving God and prayer into all situations.

Another time, when in Rome, after a long day of meetings, a group of us went out to a very popular gelato bar. The young man behind the counter was rushing to fill many orders. It was my turn, and I saw him rubbing his shoulder. I told him to catch his breath and take his time making mine since it looked like his shoulder was aching. He affirmed that it was. I felt prodded to take out a blessed Miraculous Medal from my pocket, kiss it, and reach over the counter to hand it to him. He kissed it and put it into his pocket with a smile. I told him I'd pray that his shoulder felt better.

I thank God that my daughter Mary-Catherine, a young woman in her early twenties, is becoming a woman for others. Her example of going to Mass every Sunday and holy day resonated with her two college roommates who had no religious upbringing. They started to go with her. Eventually, they expressed their desire to become Catholic! They plan to go through an RCIA program.

Another story about my daughter further illustrates this:

I sat straight up in bed at exactly three in the morning when the phone roused me out of a sound sleep. A bit startled, I grabbed it to answer.

"Mom?"

Scared to find out why she was calling me at that hour, I asked, "Are you okay?" She was in her dorm at her out-of-state college. She blurted out "yes!" fast so I wouldn't worry any further.

"For the sake of his sorrowful passion," I prayed out loud (actually in a bit of a whisper). Without missing a beat my daughter replied, "Have mercy on us and on the whole world." Since it was three o'clock, the Hour of Great Mercy, I wanted to call for Christ's mercy in that moment.

Then Mary-Catherine proceeded to tell me that a student she knew was completely drunk and she was very worried about her. She wanted to be sure she was doing all of the right things to, in essence, save her life. I tiptoed out of the bedroom and into my office to avoid disturbing my sleeping husband. I reached down to turn on my computer while I asked Mary-Catherine for more information.

As she spilled out the gory details, my heart was secretly singing praises that my daughter would feel comfortable to come to me for this kind of help. She trusted I wouldn't judge her classmate but instead would give her appropriate and sound advice. I quickly "Googled" what to do in those situations to be sure I wasn't missing something and found that what I was telling my daughter was exactly what should be done.

We agreed that she absolutely had to call for emergency medical help immediately if it was needed, not worrying about the girl getting into trouble. Her life was more precious than that. She also understood she could call me back at any time if she needed additional moral support or advice after we talked. We knew of a young man who got drunk at a house party in a nearby town and was left alone by his friends to sleep it off. The poor soul choked on his vomit and died. Mary-Catherine stayed up all night with her friend, caring for her and making sure that she would be fine. God sends us forth in all kinds of situations.

For a mother, being "sent forth" might well mean within her own home—her domestic church—in her faithfulness to care for her family and all that entails. She need not fear she isn't accomplishing much (sometimes it looks that way) because she is in reality raising her little saints to heaven. Other women might be sent forth in the workplace, the convent, the neighborhood, or the community. Wherever we find ourselves as Catholic women, we work out our salvation and help others to do so as well, within the exchanges and love we show to others.

One day a young mother named Jennifer was bubbling with excitement and shared it with me. She had been praying and striving to serve Jesus in others and told me that one of my books (*Grace Café: Serving Up Recipes for Faithful*

Mothering) prodded her to start putting her Christian love into action.

She said, "I have been praying I would find something that would inspire me to be a good Catholic mother and show me how. I cannot express in words how proud and excited I am to be Catholic—even more so now that I know what to do thanks to you and your book!"

She then told me about her moving encounter. "I think I was really paying attention today when I was at the store. You see there was an older lady who needed some help reading a price on the milk, and I don't know what got into me, but I hurried over to her as quickly as I could and helped her." Jennifer's children were in the shopping cart beside her as she reached out to the woman. "We had a really nice conversation about my kids and laundry and dishes, and before we went our separate ways she thanked me and said, 'You have a good day in Jesus' name, in Jesus' name!' I was beaming! I just knew that was him. I KNEW it! And I was able to recognize him! Your book has been a real eyeopener for me personally, and I couldn't be happier!" Jennifer really felt that she was serving Jesus within the woman she helped at the grocery store. She also set an invaluable lesson to her young children.

St. Josemaria Escrivá reminded us to be cognizant of all we do, for as Christians, we are an example of faith, hope, and love to others. He said,

> Constantly call to mind that at every moment you are cooperating in the human and spiritual formation of those around you, and of all souls—for the blessed Communion of Saints reaches as far as that. At every moment: when you work and when you rest; when people see you happy or when they see you worried; when at your job, or out in the street, you pray as does a

child of God and the peace of your soul shows through
when people see that you have suffered, that you have
wept, and you smile.[2]

This reminds me of an interesting exchange I had with
a young woman at a veterinarian's office. I brought my dog
in for a checkup and spent a bit of time alone with the technician as she administered a few tests on Sweetpea. Before
long, we were talking about kids. I told her I was a writer
and wrote for mothers, families, and women. Her language
suddenly changed, becoming less professional. More than a
few times she used the Lord's name in vain and even used
the *F* word a couple of times. So, I blessed myself with the
Sign of the Cross right in front of her. I smiled and gently
told her I did so because she was using the Lord's name
in vain. That didn't stop her from swearing, though, and I
concluded that she felt extremely comfortable with me since
she spoke so freely about her personal life, as if I was one of
her closest friends. I don't think her boss would have been
happy to hear her speak that way, but no one was with us
in the examination room to monitor. Of course, I overlooked
the cursing and listened intently as she spoke about her toddler, her five-month-old baby, and her fiancé.

The subject of prayer also came up since we were talking
about mothering. Before we parted, I gave her my business
card along with a promise to drop off one of my books for
mothers since she had expressed interest in reading one.
We never know what will happen on any given day when
we offer ourselves to God and ask him to use us to bring
others to him.

Just as I typed the last line of the paragraph above, my
telephone rang. It was a ninety-something-year-old woman
I know who lives alone. She told me she just happened
to turn on the television last night to a channel she never

watches, "and there you were!" It was an interview of me by Father Benedict Groeschel on his show *Sunday Night Prime* on EWTN. Father Benedict and I spoke about our mutual friend Blessed Mother Teresa. I should mention that this friend who called is an atheist and has made that very clear to me a few times already. But just now she said, "I can't tell you how much I enjoyed that show."

See what I mean? When we offer ourselves to God and ask him to use us to bring others to him, he hears our prayer. He is always working, always loving. He wants this woman safe with him in heaven in the not too distant future I would imagine. How wonderful that he inspired an atheist to turn the channel to a Catholic television station!

My friend on the phone asked, "How did you get into all this?" Without trying to be preachy, being sensitive to the fact that she doesn't like "preachy" since she is an atheist, I said, "Well, I always want to help people and so I asked God to use me. "There was no getting away from that fact—I had to say it. At least I didn't gush about how much I love God. She took it extremely well, though, and had more kind things to say. Her phone call to me just now was a big bright spot in my day. I'll continue to bring her homemade chicken soup (with an extra dash of love sprinkled in) and call her on the phone so she won't feel so alone and will hopefully feel Christ's love in her life. I will indeed be praying that what she "happened upon" last night on the show will have an enormous impact on her heart. I hope you'll pray for her and all those in similar situations who are unbelievers, lonely, and in need of Christ in their lives, so that someone nearby can be a light in their lives and help them get to heaven.

Here I Am, Lord, Send Me

When I ponder how we women are there for others by our loving presence, my thoughts turn immediately to the Blessed Mother, who ran in haste to help her elderly cousin Elizabeth who was pregnant. As we know, Mary was pregnant as well and was no doubt feeling a bit queasy and tired. Maybe she was still getting the hang of the gargantuan role entrusted to her to be the Mother of God. Yet, she ran to help someone else, being a faithful "woman for others." We'll be discussing the Blessed Mother in great depth in our last chapter, "My Soul Magnifies the Lord."

Some Catholic women worry that God can't "send" them out because they are housebound with kids, illness, care of elderly relatives, and other responsibilities. Truth be told, they are already being "sent" right where they are. And if the good Lord wants someone in your life that particular day, he'll send them to you!

As I was writing this chapter and waiting for my carton of *Bringing Lent Home with Mother Teresa* books to arrive so that I could fill orders, the delivery truck pulled into my driveway. I went down to open the door for the delivery. The fellow carrying the box had a nice, dark, black cross on his forehead. Yes, I said "forehead"!

"Oh, you're wearing your ashes?" I exuberantly asked.

"Yes—got them at Mass this morning!"

I told him I'd be getting mine tonight, since it's Ash Wednesday, and also said, "Well, you know the box you're carrying is filled with Lenten books. If you give me a second, I'll go grab a knife to open the box and give you one." Well, he pulled out a knife and opened the box for me. As he did we quickly shared where we go to church. I grabbed a book and a pen, and signed a book to Gerry. He was surprised to come across an author in his journey.

Delivery guys are always in a rush to make their good timing on deliveries, but I ventured to ask if I could run upstairs to get him something. Since he was fine with it, I did and came back downstairs with four blessed Miraculous Medals for him, his wife, and two grown children whom he said still go to Mass. These were special medals that I had placed on Blessed Pope John Pau II's tomb and Blessed Mother Teresa's bed at the convent where she stayed with the sisters when she was in Rome. He was extremely thankful. I said, "Good thing you had your ashes on! See how good God is, to make this all happen?" He wholeheartedly agreed. "He always is," he said with the biggest smile as he headed back to his truck. Truth be told, ashes on someone's forehead are not required for me to venture to give someone a blessed medal or a book!

Another time, prior to one of my speaking events, a very large book order arrived at my house. The delivery man felt comfortable enough when chatting with me as he wheeled boxes of books to my door that he paused to open his shirt and show me the scar from a very recent pacemaker insertion. Initially, he was in a big rush and appeared stressed. He wanted to leave the ten heavy boxes in my driveway. Since it was beginning to rain and I knew I couldn't manage to bring the boxes in myself, I hurried out to his truck as he started to pull away, waving my arms to get his attention so I could ask for his help. He said he feared he wouldn't get his other deliveries completed because he was given a heavy schedule that day and he didn't have a hand truck on his truck. But, as I spoke to him, he seemed to calm down. I told him I had a hand truck in the garage that we could use. He shut off the truck engine and helped me with the numerous boxes.

Since it was raining, I invited him into my foyer to finish our conversation. We chatted about illness, faith, and prayer, and I promised my prayers for him and gave him a couple of my books and a blessed Miraculous Medal to send him on his way. That previously stressed-out man, who had been in such a rush, left my home with a happy and peaceful demeanor, shaking his head in disbelief and saying, "This stop was really meant to be, and I never get this route. Thank you!" Life is exciting when you pray to serve the Lord.

Recently a woman named Julie shared a story with me about a time when she felt God had given her "an important opportunity" to be a "woman for others." She told me she often prays that God would keep her "alert to the opportunities he presents" so she can "help others and give him glory." She explained that she constantly desires to be "his hands, his feet, his voice." Because she never wants to miss his calls to her, she prays daily that her "ears will hear his voice" and her "heart will be open to his every grace."

Julie volunteered to bring a home-cooked dinner to Anne and her family. Anne was a woman from her parish who was recuperating from amputation surgery. Julie's heart went out to Anne and was pleased she could help in some way. As Julie prepared the meal, breaking up the bread for the croutons and tossing them in olive oil, she prayed that the dinner she prepared would nourish the family. "I remember feeling love for the family and wanting them to enjoy the dinner," she said.

But her normally happy toddler was napless and cranky and wouldn't stop tugging on her pant leg while she was trying to make the homemade garlic croutons for the arugula salad. Earlier, her one-year-old was a handful in the grocery store, and Julie just about gave up on the idea and thought she might have to switch the day with someone else because it was beginning to be so difficult to pull off. She was thinking, "How am I going to get dinner ready and delivered on time?" She started to stress out and feel a little annoyed, but then she quickly caught herself. She didn't want to be doing a work of mercy with a stressed attitude. "This isn't the kind of heart Jesus wanted me to have while preparing the dinner for them. He wanted me to do it with love." She reminded herself, "God knows how much I can carry." So, she prayed, "God, help me, please!" And he did.

Julie's husband came to the rescue by helping with the three young children as well as with the pasta dinner Julie was trying to make. Things began to settle down. When it was time to deliver the meal, Julie headed out to Anne's house. But halfway there she felt a sudden compelling urge to turn around and go back home to get something. When one of the kids began to complain, Julie almost second-guessed her decision to retrieve the blessed Miraculous Medal that she received in the mail from me that day along with her book order. She wanted to give it to Anne along with a bookmark with the beautiful verse "Come to me, all you that are weary and are carrying heavy burdens, and I will give you rest. Take my yoke upon you, and learn from me; for I am gentle and humble in heart, and you will find rest for your souls. For my yoke is easy, and my burden is light" (Mt 11:28–30). Julie took a moment to quiet her son and explain the importance of helping and loving others in need, even if it's inconvenient. Julie managed to deliver the meal on time to a very appreciative family. The next morning, after dropping her third grader off at school, she settled into her pew at morning Mass. She said she was stunned when she heard the monsignor say that they would be praying for Anne who passed that morning. "I thought I heard it wrong at first, but it was true."

It was so hard to believe. Julie had just visited with her only hours before. She told me, "I felt compelled to follow up with you and share the story, because often we never know how a simple act of kindness can have such a ripple effect of goodness all around us." She explained, "Because you sent that Miraculous Medal, because you sent the package so promptly, by God's amazing timing I was able to give her that spiritual nourishment, along with the physical nourishment of her last dinner."

Julie was touched that Anne's husband Gary, whom Julie barely knew, called her later that day. After just losing his wife and being suddenly left with a young daughter to raise alone, he took time out of his intense grief to thank Julie and let her know that the medal and the bookmark meant a great deal to him.

A couple of days later, Julie felt a surge of peace come to her heart as she heard the same gospel words at Anne's memorial Mass: "Come to me, all you that are weary and are carrying heavy burdens, and I will give you rest. Take my yoke upon you, and learn from me; for I am gentle and humble in heart, and you will find rest for your souls. For my yoke is easy, and my burden is light."

Julie shared, "After Mass, Gary found me and gave me a giant hug. He thanked me, again and said, 'You know, those words are the last thing she read.'" Julie continued, "Also, Donna-Marie, you probably know this, but I . . . just learned . . . that graces for a 'happy death' are attached to the Miraculous Medal."

Julie said she is often "amazed at Divine Providence, and God's attention to every detail in our lives." She feels very relieved and happy that she prayed for God's help not to bow out but instead to be able to carry out her "important opportunity" to be Jesus' hands and feet to others in need.

Of course, as with everything else we do, we need to first create a firm foundation of prayer in our lives in order to do the work—to answer God's invitation to be sent forth. In his encyclical letter *Deus Caritas Est* (*God Is Love*), Pope Benedict XVI reminded us about the importance of grounding ourselves with prayer before setting out to help our neighbor:

> In the example of Blessed Teresa of Calcutta we have a
> clear illustration of the fact that time devoted to God in
> prayer not only does not distract from effective and lov-
> ing service to our neighbor but is in fact the inexhaust-
> ible source of that service. (*DCE* 36)

Blessed Mother Teresa pointed out very clearly that her work was not merely social service. It was holy work that required prayer, the sacraments (which I mentioned earlier), and an awareness of Jesus' call to serve him in one another (which we'll get into in more depth in our next chapter). For now, as Catholic women, we'll be cognizant that we too have the responsibility to establish a meaningful prayer life in order to do the work that God has commissioned to us. Naturally, we won't always know what the commission might be. And it can change on any given day. Yet, our Lord wants us to put one foot in front of the other in faith each day to follow him. He'll show us the way and provide countless opportunities for us to serve others with his love. The more we pray, the more Jesus will live and shine through us and others will be helped.

I'd like to share a very special prayer with you that was one of Mother Teresa's favorites. She and her sisters prayed it each day after receiving Holy Communion. It was written by John Henry Newman (an Anglican priest who converted to Catholicism in 1845 and was beatified by Pope Benedict XVI on September 19, 2010). Perhaps you can find some time to pray it each day, too.

Radiating Christ
Dear Jesus, help me to spread Your fragrance every-
where I go.
Flood my soul with Your spirit and life.
Penetrate and possess my whole being so utterly that
all my life may only be a radiance of Yours.

Shine through me and be so in me that every soul I
    come in contact with may feel Your presence in
    my soul.
Let them look up and see no longer me but only Jesus!
Stay with me and then I shall begin to shine as you
    shine,
so to shine as to be a light to others; the light, O Jesus,
    will be all from you;
none of it will be mine: it will be you shining on others
    through me.
Let me thus praise you in the way you love best: by
    shining on those around me.
Let me preach you without preaching, not by words,
    but by my example,
by the catching force, the sympathetic influence of
    what I do,
the evident fullness of the love my heart bears to you.
    Amen.

A MOMENT TO REFLECT

Our lives are so rich and filled with wonderful encounters
with the people we interact with, all because of God's providence. At times, it might seem that nothing noteworthy is
happening in our lives, but we shouldn't worry. As long
as we have prayed and asked our Lord to use us to be that
woman for others, he certainly will.

At times, our ministering to others is in the simplicity of
our loving smile, through the gentle care of our hands, and
through offered prayers from our hearts. At other times, it
will come across in more dramatic ways. Each way is powerful and vital. We leave it all up to God and ask him to do
the work through us.

Let's ask the Holy Spirit to guide us in our prayer lives,
giving us the inspiration and push we need to "be not

afraid" (as Blessed John Paul II was famous for saying) to go forth as a "woman for others" in whatever that might mean in our state of life.

My Mind to Know Him

1. Calling to mind the words from St. Francis de Sales, what kind of tapestry are you "embroidering"?

2. Can you take a few minutes sometime soon to ponder the virtues you might want to practice?

3. Earlier in the chapter I quoted Blessed John Paul II : when "like Moses we say: 'Here I am,' then he reveals more clearly both himself and his compassionate love for his people in need. Gradually he leads us to discover the practical way in which we should serve him: 'I will send you.'" Can you take some time to prayerfully think about the practical way our Lord might be asking you to serve him?

My Heart to Love Him

1. In your prayers, can you ask God how he is expecting you to be a "woman for others"?

2. When time allows, can you list three ideas for serving someone close to you in a tangible way?

3. Also, list three ways you can serve someone in a silent but loving way.

My Hands to Serve Him

1. The next time you do a task, whatever it is, pray silently as you do it. If it's for someone else, pray for them as you carry it out.

2. Depending on your state in life, can you join forces with another woman or two and do some sort of charitable service for someone you know in need?

3. Can you think of someone in your life that can use cheering up and secretly do something to help him or her in that regard?

Seeking God

Dear Lord, thank you for the awesome mission of being a Catholic woman. Help me to serve you in all I come in contact with. With your love, help me to bring others closer to you. Amen.

9.

WHEN DID
I SEE YOU, LORD?

The love of Christ urges us on.

—2 Corinthians 5:14

Most likely you have been to church during a holy day or feast day when blessed incense is used. Billows of smoke reach up from the censer and waft all around the church while the intense aroma surrounds us. Sometimes it even makes us cough. But it's very ceremonial; it's holy—it helps draw us into the proper prayerful frame of mind as our prayers ascend to God like the incense.

St. Paul uses the analogy of incense to illustrate who we are in the world:

> But thanks be to God, who in Christ always leads us in triumphal procession, and through us spreads in every place the fragrance that comes from knowing him. For we are the aroma of Christ to God among those who are being saved and among those who are perishing; to the one a fragrance from death to death, to the other a fragrance from life to life. . . . In Christ we speak as persons of sincerity, as persons sent from God and standing in his presence. (2 Cor 2:14–17)

159

We, in essence, are holy incense to others—the "aroma of Christ." How? By living a faithful Catholic life. Through our prayers, by following the commandments, and by frequenting the sacraments, we, with God's grace, become that holy aroma. And, with a womanly desiring heart, we reach out to help others, our brothers and sisters who are in need, whether spiritually or physically.

Remember our Lord's "instruction booklet" to get us to heaven?

> "You shall love the Lord your God with all your heart, and with all your soul, and with all your mind." This is the greatest and first commandment. And a second is like it: "You shall love your neighbor as yourself." On these two commandments hang all the law and the prophets. (Mt 22:37–40)

We are fortunate that God has given us very clear instructions. Let's keep these vital directives fresh in our minds. Throughout this chapter, we'll explore ways in which we love God and our neighbor through our caring hearts and hands.

Not to heap undue stress and fear upon you, dear sister in Christ, but I do have to tell the whole story. I can't just write a warm and fuzzy book that won't challenge you to follow our Lord precisely in the way he calls you as a Catholic woman. Jesus did not mince words regarding how we will all be judged at the end of our lives and how we will be punished eternally if we have not taken care of those who are needy.

Unambiguous Divine Instructions

Our Lord warned,

> Then he will say to those at his left hand, "You that are
> accursed, depart from me into the eternal fire prepared
> for the devil and his angels; for I was hungry and you
> gave me no food, I was thirsty and you gave me noth-
> ing to drink, I was a stranger and you did not welcome
> me, naked and you did not give me clothing, sick and in
> prison and you did not visit me." (Mt 25:41–43)

Jesus explains what we must do to inherit the kingdom
of heaven. I love this part of scripture and even have it book-
marked with a picture of Blessed Mother Teresa in my Bible
to hold this spot. You'll see why in a minute. Please read
Matthew 25:31–46 when you can. Since it's long, I will quote
a portion of it.

> Come, you that are blessed by my Father, inherit the
> kingdom prepared for you from the foundation of the
> world; for I was hungry and you gave me food, I was
> thirsty and you gave me something to drink, I was a
> stranger and you welcomed me, I was naked and you
> gave me clothing, I was sick and you took care of me,
> I was in prison and you visited me. . . . Truly I tell you,
> just as you did it to one of the least of these who are
> members of my family, you did it to me. (Mt 25:34–36,
> 40)

Within the passage (verses 37–39, not quoted above), it
says, "Lord, when was it that we saw you hungry?" which
illustrates the "righteous" questioning our Lord when he
tells those who did not take care of him that they are going
to hell. The question from the "righteous" sounds like a
bunch of excuses rolled into an "innocent" question, and

that's what we do—we make excuses or we fail to recognize that we are to serve our Lord in everyone we meet. *Lord, when was it that we saw you? Maybe I missed you when I was watching so many reality shows and soap operas or when I was playing with my computer.* Our laziness or lack of love in our hearts causes us to take easy ways out and to make far too many excuses.

Blessed Mother Teresa lived the message in these words every day in her care for the poorest of the poor. She took these words quite literally, as we should in whatever that means to us in our particular walk of life as a Catholic woman.

We are reminded of our duty to share our goods and love in both the Old and New Testaments. We are given instructions regarding our responsibility to care for the poor and needy. In the Old Testament, we read in Isaiah,

> Is it not to share your bread with the hungry, and bring the homeless poor into your house; when you see the naked, to cover them, and not to hide yourself from your own kin? Then your light shall break forth like the dawn, and your healing shall spring up quickly; your vindicator shall go before you, the glory of the Lord shall be your rear guard. Then you shall call, and the Lord will answer; you shall cry for help, and he will say, Here I am. (Is 58:7–9)

In the New Testament we read,

> Let mutual love continue. Do not neglect to show hospitality to strangers, for by doing that some have entertained angels without knowing it. Remember those who are in prison, as though you were in prison with them; those who are being tortured, as though you yourselves were being tortured. (Heb 13:1–3)

Surprise, Surprise!

It might come as a surprise (maybe even a shock) to some, but our Church teaches that we don't actually *own* anything. In other words, what is ours is for everyone. We have to share to help others. For instance, let's ponder the following words: "What good is it, my brothers and sisters, if you say you have faith but do not have works? Can faith save you? If a brother or sister is naked and lacks daily food, and one of you says to them, 'Go in peace; keep warm and eat your fill,' and yet you do not supply their bodily needs, what is the good of that? So faith by itself, if it has no works, is dead" (Jas 2:14–17).

I love what comes next. "But someone will say, 'You have faith and I have works.' Show me your faith apart from works, and I by my works will show you my faith. . . . For just as the body without the spirit is dead, so faith without works is also dead" (Jas 2:18, 26). We can ponder these words and examine our own lives. Is my faith apparent through my works? It should be. Not that we're going to go around and boast about our good works or jump up on the nearest table and start shouting out scriptures. Yet, the wonderful thing is that, when we do works of charity for others, Christ's light shines through us. So, in addition to people benefiting by our spiritual or corporal work, their souls will also be nourished. We're taking care of the whole person—heart, mind, body, and soul. And there's more—our souls are nourished in the process!

When we do good works the goodness will come to the light of faith. St. John tells us, "But those who do what is true come to the light, so that it may be clearly seen that their deeds have been done in God" as opposed to what he said about evil doers who "hate the light and do not come to the light, so that their deeds may not be exposed" (Jn 3:21).

St. John Chrysostom was very clear about our duty to give: "Not to enable the poor to share in our goods is to steal from them and deprive them of life. The goods we possess are not ours, but theirs." And "the demands of justice must be satisfied first of all; that which is already due in justice is not offered as a gift of charity." St. Gregory the Great adds, "When we attend to the needs of those in want, we give them what is theirs, not ours. More than performing works of mercy, we are paying a debt of justice" (both quoted in CCC 2446). Those words indeed deserve pondering.

HOW WE DO IT

To put into practice all of what I have said about loving God and neighbor, I'd like to speak about the spiritual and corporal works of mercy as ways in which we can fulfill our responsibilities as Catholic women to see our Lord in others and to serve him there. The works of mercy answer the call in the Gospel of Matthew, "The Last Judgment." The corporal works take care of physical needs, while the spiritual works naturally take care of one's spiritual needs. The *Catechism* tells us, "The works of mercy are charitable actions by which we come to the aid of our neighbor in his spiritual and bodily necessities" (CCC 2447).

Corporal Works of Mercy

> Feed the hungry.
> Give drink to the thirsty.
> Clothe the naked.
> Shelter the homeless.
> Visit the sick.
> Visit the imprisoned.
> Bury the dead.

Spiritual Works of Mercy

Admonish the sinner.
Instruct the ignorant.
Counsel the doubtful.
Comfort the sorrowful.
Bear wrongs patiently.
Forgive all injuries.
Pray for the living and the dead.

"Among all these, giving alms to the poor is one of the chief witnesses to fraternal charity: it is also a work of justice pleasing to God" (CCC 2447). When you have a few quiet moments, read through these works of mercy again, and pray about how you might carry some out. I'm sure you will realize ways that you already carry some of them out and might also become inspired about how you can engage in others.

St. Thomas Aquinas taught that mercy is a spontaneous act of charity—it comes from our hearts. Pope Benedict XVI reminded us about the constant need to ease suffering. In *Deus Caritas Est*, he said, "There will always be suffering which cries out for consolation and help. There will always be situations of material need where help in the form of concrete love of neighbor is indispensable" (*DCE* 28).

In that same document, Pope Benedict XVI stated, "Love of neighbor, grounded in the love of God, is first and foremost a responsibility for each individual member of the faithful." He went on to explain that it is also the responsibility of the entire Church to love and care for neighbor. He put in plain words that human beings need more than technical professional care. "They need humanity. They need heartfelt concern" (*DCE* 31).

So, in addition to the training charity workers certainly require, Pope Benedict said "they need to be led to that encounter with God in Christ which awakens their love and opened their spirits to others." Because of that divine encounter, "love of neighbor will no longer be for them a commandment imposed, so to speak, from without, but a consequence deriving from their faith, a faith which becomes active through love (*DCE* 31; cf. Gal 5:6).

He reminds us again of the need for works of mercy. "Following the example given in the parable of the Good Samaritan, Christian charity is first of all the simple response to immediate needs and specific situations: feeding the hungry, clothing the naked, caring for and healing the sick, visiting those in prison, etc." (*DCE* 31).

We can learn so much about loving and service by looking at the lives of the saints. Pope Benedict XVI said,

> The figures of the saints such as Francis of Assisi, Ignatius of Loyola, John of God, Camillus of Lellis, Vincent de Paul, Louise de Marillac, Giuseppe B. Cottolengo, John Bosco, Luigi Orione, Teresa of Calcutta, to name a few—stand out as lasting models of social charity for all people of good will. The saints are the true bearers of light within history, for they are men and women of faith, hope, and love. (*DCE* 40)

Speaking of direction from the saints, St. Vincent de Paul said, "We should strive to keep our hearts open to the sufferings and wretchedness of other people, and pray continually that God may grant us that spirit of compassion which is truly the spirit of God." Indeed, we need to pray for guidance from the Holy Spirit regarding what works of mercy we can put into practice with heartfelt concern to benefit others around us.

Works into Action

We read in *Familiaris Consortio* that "love is the fundamental and innate vocation of every human being" (*FC* 11). And as St. Thomas Aquinas told us, mercy comes spontaneously from our hearts. So, usually our mercy toward others occurs very naturally as we recognize a need and with God's grace act upon it. Even the act of cooking a meal for our family, when done with love and prayer, is raised to a supernatural level pleasing to God. In addition, we need to pray about these needs and ask God what he wants us to do in the not so obvious situations.

Let's talk about the spontaneous acts of mercy. I'll use a few personal stories to illustrate. The first story will illustrate the work of mercy for counseling the doubtful. One time I was returning to the United States from a conference in Rome, Italy, and had to wait in an extraordinarily lengthy line at a Rome airport. I began chatting with a couple in front of me. The subject of the Catholic Church came up, and the gentleman told me he thought everything in the controversial book *The Da Vinci Code* was true! His wife was an Anglican. I did my best for the three-hour wait in line to defend the Church and "counsel the doubtful."

I finally boarded the plane and got seated. Unbeknown to me, I was in for a very harrowing flight. The plane went through terrible turbulence for a good part of the flight. It was frightening for many. I was indeed praying. A couple of times it seemed we might not make it to the United States! The first period of turbulence occurred right at takeoff when the plane shook violently from side to side.

A young woman seated across the aisle from me began to hyperventilate. I naturally reached out my hand to stroke her arm and told her it would be okay. I offered her my Rosary, with which I had been praying. She happily accepted it and drew it immediately to her heart. I dug into my carry-on bag and retrieved a blessed Miraculous Medal that Blessed Mother Teresa had given me.

The young woman took the medal and attached it to the long, fashionable Italian chain she was wearing. She held the medal in one hand and the Rosary in the other. She let out a big sigh and calmed down. She seemed to take great comfort in these sacramentals. We chatted, and the older woman sitting in the seat next to her looked on intently. I talked to this young woman about prayer, God, our Blessed Mother, Blessed Mother Teresa, and the saints. She was intrigued and nodded continuously as she took it all in and asked if she could hold onto my Rosary throughout the flight.

Later on when the plane stopped rocking, an elderly man who was sitting two rows behind me on the right leaned toward me, tapped me on the arm, and whispered, "How did you do that?" For a second I wondered what he could have meant. He must have detected a puzzled look from me. "You helped that girl; how did you do that?" I replied, "God put a lot of love in my heart. I like to help people." That was the very simple way I could express it to that curious man. Notice that I got God into our conversation? He seemed very touched, right through to his core. He wiped a tear from his eye.

You know who else was watching? The *Da Vinci Code* couple! We are the "aroma" of our Church wherever we are. Our reaching out in love to comfort somebody helps not only that person but also those who observe.

The young lady told me that her name was Federica and she was twenty-six years old. We exchanged contact information. After that long flight, Federica held me tight in an embrace when we got up to get off the plane in New York. Before we parted ways, she told me that I was welcome anytime to stay at her home in Rome. The woman who was

sitting near her turned out to be her mother. She also gave
me a hug, and then they were off to tour NYC for the week.
After I got home and unpacked, I sent Federica a Rosary
that I had bought in Rome and that was blessed by Pope
Benedict. I pray it brings her many blessings.

This next story will speak of visiting the sick and praying
for the living and the dead. On my birthday several years
ago, I visited my older brother Gary, who was in hospice
care at an out-of-state facility due to cancer that had mercilessly ravaged his body. He had just slipped into a coma. I
noticed that his face was hot and feverish upon arriving to
his room, and I loosened his blankets and called his nurse.
She administered a fever reducer and then left me and my
family alone to visit with Gary. I washed my brother's face
gently with a cool washcloth as I prayed for him and held
back some tears. That terrible disease of cancer had robbed
this good man of a longer life. I took out my brown scapular
and blessed Gary with the Sign of the Cross on his forehead.
My family and I kept vigil at his bedside and prayed for him
until it was time to head for home. The next morning I called
to check on Gary to see if his fever had gone away. I was told
that my brother had died. I cried but was very thankful I
had visited him one last time here on earth and that he had
received the anointing of the sick by a priest before he died.

Years later, I heard that a relative of my ex-husband (I'll
call him Andrew) was in the hospital with cancer. I hadn't
seen or heard from him in about twenty-five years. He was
an over-the-road truck driver. I was in communication
with his mother, so we arranged to go over to the hospital
together to see him. I was happy that Andrew was not only
okay with my visit but also welcomed it. I continued to
visit him throughout the next couple of months, bringing
homemade chicken soup and oatmeal raisin cookies, and I
called him on the phone almost every day.

The cancer was ferocious, and Andrew's once strong body was withering away fast. When I was alone with him, I began asking him if he ever prayed. I was well aware of the kind of wild life he had led up until this point, and it didn't seem that prayer would be a part of it. So each day, I ventured further and further with our spiritual conversations; I let him know I was praying for him and in a gentle way told him he needed to prepare his soul to meet God. He told me he was now praying.

Andrew started to slip into a coma shortly after our prayer conversations. One day I, along with his mother, went to see Andrew. I usually walked his mom out to her car when she finished her visits, but this day I told her I would stay a while longer. I looked at the clock. It was about 2:45 p.m. I pulled out my beads and began to pray the Divine Mercy chaplet for the sick and dying.

Jesus had asked St. Faustina to pray the Divine Mercy chaplet especially for sinners and the dying. It is quoted in her *Diary* (the book she wrote recounting Jesus' instructions to her) that Jesus said to her,

> Pray as much as you can for the dying. By your entreaties [that is, insistent prayers] obtain for them trust in My mercy, because they have most need of trust, and have it the least. Be assured that the grace of eternal salvation for certain souls in their final moment depends on your prayer. You know the whole abyss of My mercy, so draw upon it for yourself and especially for poor sinners. Sooner would heaven and earth turn into nothingness than would My mercy not embrace a trusting soul.[1]

Jesus also told St. Faustina,

> My daughter, encourage souls to say the chaplet which I have given you. It pleases Me to grant everything they

ask of Me by saying the chaplet. . . . Write that when they
say this chaplet in the presence of the dying, I will stand
between My Father and the dying person, not as the just
Judge but as the merciful Savior.[2]

I prayed the chaplet as Andrew lay unconscious and
finished at 3:00 p.m., the Hour of Great Mercy. I made the
Sign of the Cross on Andrew's forehead and stayed a little
longer by his side. Before heading home, I kissed Andrew
"good-bye." I knew I wouldn't be seeing him again this
side of heaven. I got word later confirming my forethought.
Andrew had passed away only a couple of hours after my
visit.

Afterward, at Andrew's wake and funeral, Andrew's
truck driver friends, whom I had met in the hospital during
many visits, came up to me to thank me for my presence in
Andrew's life. Most of them led the same kind of wild life
of drugs and alcohol that Andrew had led, and they seemed
to be touched deeply by God's love.

Imagine my excitement a couple of years later as I stood
at the front of my parish church during Mass as an extraordinary minister of Holy Communion. One of Matt's friends
whom I had met at the hospital stood before me and raised
up his hands as a throne to receive Jesus in Holy Communion. My heart was rejoicing!

The above story illustrates "praying for the living and the
dead" and "visiting the sick." As Catholics, we help when
we are able, even when it is inconvenient. We endeavor to
comfort the dying emotionally and physically as well as
minister to their spiritual needs (which can include making
sure they get an Anointing of the Sick if it is appropriate to
their situation). We also want to be a holy presence to their
family members and friends. God will work through us if
we allow him to.

The following story illustrates "comforting the sorrowful," a work of mercy—being present, helping,—taking
time to listen to someone hurting in some way. On one of
my flights down to the EWTN studio in Alabama to record
new segments for my television show *Everyday Blessings for
Catholic Moms*, I had a very out-of-the-ordinary encounter. I
sat near a young woman who seemed occupied with reading
her magazine, so other than a quick, polite hello, I didn't get
involved in a conversation with her, assuming she wanted
some privacy. I prayed my Rosary silently. It would be about
a three-hour flight.

I always pray before traveling, not only for safe travel
but also for God to put me next to whomever he wants
me to be with. Then I like to pray the Rosary upon takeoff
and landing. About halfway through the flight, the pilot
announced we would land about fifty minutes early. Suddenly, disrupted from her reading, the woman beside me
turned to me and asked, "Did he say fifteen minutes or
fifty?" I confirmed his words and so the ice was broken. We
then began a conversation.

By the grace of God, somehow we got to talking about
faith! Right now, I can't remember how that happened.
Sometimes I can never quite remember how the amazing
encounters with which God blesses me are initiated. It is
quite amazing how perfect strangers start talking about
God. He sets up the opportunities, and I praise him for it.

So, the young woman, whose name was Nancy, and I
began an interesting conversation. I felt compelled to reach
into my pocket to retrieve the blessed Miraculous Medal I
had put in there that morning before heading out, when I
felt confident it might very well find a home around someone's neck sometime that day (please God!).

As I took the medal out and handed it to her, I said I
wanted to give her something that I felt was very special.

I proceeded to tell her it was blessed and that I had placed it on Pope John Paul II's tomb at the Vatican and also on Blessed Mother Teresa's bed at the convent where she stayed when she was in Rome with the Missionary of Charity sisters. I then kissed it and touched it to the medal I wear that Mother Teresa had given me. I handed it to her. She was so visibly happy to receive it.

She said, "Oh! You have no idea how much this means to me!" She reached around her neck to take off her chain and then put the blessed Miraculous Medal on her necklace. I was so happy that she would actually wear it because the Blessed Mother had stated to St. Catherine Labouré, to whom she appeared in Paris, that those who *wear* the medal will receive many graces.

Specifically, in 1830, after showing St. Catherine Labouré a vision of the image of the medal, Mary said, "Have a medal struck upon this model. All who wear it, when it is blessed, will receive great graces, especially if they wear it around the neck."

As Nancy placed the medal around her neck she said she was Methodist (and still welcomed the medal!) and then told me her amazing story. It was about a month and a half earlier when something frightening but profound had happened to her. I was on the edge of my seat in anticipation, inwardly praising Jesus for this encounter and asking dear Mary to intercede, all the while listening to each word.

On what should have been an ordinary work morning, Nancy was in her kitchen in Alabama making the sandwich she would bring to work for lunch. Her two housemates had just left for work and she was to be leaving shortly.

This was during the time of the fierce killer tornados that had been ruthlessly hitting that area. The sirens began wailing, and Nancy listened intently to the radio, in between the blasts of the sirens and the roars of the wind, to know what she should do.

The wind all of a sudden seemed to be knocking fiercely at her door for she heard startling intense thumping sounds right near her at the back door. Before she could react in any way, the door came crashing in!

What she did not expect to see was the hoodlum who had broken her door down. He immediately grabbed her and started to pound on her head. After what seemed like an eternity of brutal abuse, the intruder told her to move to the bedroom. He pushed her small frame toward her bedroom.

Nancy cried out from the depths of her heart, "Jesus! In the name of Jesus, leave!" Over and over again, she cried out her mantra. Suddenly, an idea struck her: jewelry! "I have jewelry!" she shouted. "Where?" he wanted to know.

She showed him her jewelry box in her room. As he reached for it, she managed to escape and ran all the way to her neighbor's house, pounding on the door to get in. Once safely inside, she blurted out what had just happened, and her neighbor grabbed his shotgun and fired a few shots toward the robber, who was now fleeing the scene with her jewelry box.

Nancy didn't care if he got away with her things; she was just so relieved that she was able to escape and that God had spared her further harm. However, the gunshots startled the robber, and he dropped the jewelry box and fled. So Nancy never lost her jewelry.

As she told me the story, Nancy rested one hand against her heart and softly let the words come out, seeming to feel it all over again. I told her she need not recount such a frightening and painful experience. But she told me it was okay. She wanted to. She said she was doing very well, and it was fine to talk about it.

Nancy moved her bangs aside and showed me the scar on her forehead; she also pointed to the back of her head where numerous staple sutures were required to close her head injuries. She explained that the experience somehow miraculously brought her even closer to God. She said she had been searching and praying deeply prior to that incident. Nancy carefully pulled out her Bible from the pocket of the seat in front of her and let it sit on her lap as she spoke to me. She said she forgave the man for what he had done, but it was very hard for her family to understand how she could.

After expressing my sorrow to her that she had to go through that horrendous beating and frightful experience, I told her that I was so thankful to God she was okay now and that God was blessing her (maybe more than she could imagine). I expressed my happiness that we had met by God's providence and could talk and share our faith.

I said I just loved how God sets up these encounters and that I give him all the glory. She agreed wholeheartedly. I shared with her that I pray when I travel and ask the Lord to place me where he wants me to be and use me for his glory. She told me that she would start praying about her seating now. And I told her that, even if we don't ask God, we need not worry; he'll do it anyway. He's in control—of everything!

Our beautiful conversation continued, and we were so very thankful to God for his mysterious ways and his great love for us all. We decided to have our photo taken with my iPhone after we got out of the plane. We'd find someone there in the airport to snap it. We exchanged contact information and, after the photo was taken, parted with a big hug. God is so very good to us!

To think that, had Nancy continued with her magazine reading and had I not ventured to bring up the subject of faith, we might never have experienced our amazing

sharing, and she wouldn't be wearing that blessed Miraculous Medal. But God always has a plan, and his graces
abound. I pray that our dear Mother Mary is watching over
Nancy, too. *"O Mary conceived without sin, pray for us who
have recourse to thee"* (inscription on the Miraculous Medal).

Regarding our responsibility to love our neighbor, Father
Hardon said,

> According to St. John Chrysostom, on the Last Day,
> we shall be judged mainly on our practice of charity in
> spreading the faith. The number of ways of spreading
> the faith is beyond human reckoning. But the one way
> that has been most effective from the dawn of Christian
> history has been by living a life of selfless charity. The
> charity of which we are speaking is not only, or even
> mainly, the charity of the corporal works of mercy. Cer-
> tainly, as Christ tells us, we are to do everything we can
> to feed the hungry, give drink to the thirsty, clothe the
> naked, visit the sick, and care for those who are in physi-
> cal need. However, the principal form of charity, which
> is nothing less than a miraculous means of spreading the
> faith, is the interior charity of selfless love for others. No
> one has improved on the description of charity of Pope
> Clement I, writing in 90 AD. "Charity," he says, "bears
> all things. Charity is longsuffering in all things. There
> is nothing mean in charity, nothing arrogant. Charity
> knows no schism, does not rebel, does all things in con-
> cord. In charity, all the elect of God have been made
> perfect."[3]

Let's definitely pray for an increase in our hearts of that
amazing virtue of love that "bears all things" as well as a
greater awareness of the needs of others in our midst. God
always has a divine plan, and we are a part of it when we
surrender our hearts to him.

I must tell you something very heartening. Remember the ninety-something-year-old shut-in woman I told you about in the last chapter who was amazed to see me on EWTN? On one of my visits to her after she had seen the show, she asked me to talk with her more about my life and my ministry as a Catholic woman. We had a very nice conversation, and when I was leaving she said, "I wish I could have recorded everything you have just said. It was incredible!" I gave her a hug and kiss good-bye, and she held my hands, looked me straight in the eyes, and said, "Please continue your prayers for me." I reassured her I would and told her I loved her and that God loves her, too. After I left I continued to thank God for his amazing love and grace—a self-professed atheist was asking for prayers—amazing!

I wholeheartedly believe that our works of mercy must always be carried out with a loving and sincere heart; otherwise, we won't accomplish anything and might even turn people away from God. The very reason this woman told me on several occasions that she was an unbeliever is because she said she was being preached at by some people in her life and she didn't like it one bit. She didn't feel love from them, only condemnation, and because of it, feared further preaching. Christ's love, compassion, and chicken soup work wonders!

St. Thérèse of Lisieux has said, "I know of no other means to reach perfection than by love. To love: how perfectly our hearts are made for this! Sometimes I look for another word to use, but, in this land of exile, no other word expresses so well the vibrations of our soul. Hence we must keep to that one word: love."

Let's keep "that one word: love" ever ready on our hearts, lips, and hands to go forth and minister to all we meet as the holy aroma of our Church "for we are the aroma of Christ" (2 Cor 2:15).

A MOMENT TO REFLECT

As Catholic women, we find ourselves in a myriad of situations, meshed in the lives of countless people from family to strangers with whom we connect by God's grace. We strive to practice the virtues and pray for an increase in them so we can please God, love him, and love our neighbor. We begin to discover God working in our lives and become more cognizant that he is counting on us to draw others closer to him through our faithful lives.

St. Augustine told us, "Love is itself the fulfillment of all our works. There is the goal; that is why we run; we run towards it, and once we reach it, in it we shall find rest" (CCC 1829).

My Mind to Know Him

1. Stop to think about the following words in Matthew: "Truly I tell you, just as you did it to one of the least of these who are members of my family, you did it to me" (Mt 25:40).

2. Can you list three ways you see Jesus in others on a daily basis?

3. Can you list three ways you can begin to see Jesus in others in a manner you have not done before?

My Heart to Love Him

1. Pray and ask God to guide you and strengthen you in your resolve to love him and your neighbor even more.

2. Is there someone in your life who is "pushing your buttons" and with whom you are unhappy? Can you go out of your way to be Christ's love to him or her?

3. Can you add a few minutes to your daily prayer sched-
    ule to pray for the dying? Here is a prayer you can say:

    > O most merciful Jesus, lover of souls, I beseech thee,
    > by the agony of thy Most Sacred Heart and by the sor-
    > rows of Thine immaculate Mother, wash clean in thy
    > Blood the sinners of the whole world who are now in
    > their agony and who are to die this day. Amen. Heart
    > of Jesus, who didst suffer death's agony, have Mercy
    > on the dying.[4]

    You can also pray the Divine Mercy chaplet for the
    dying.

My Hands to Serve Him

1. Look at the list of spiritual and corporal works of mercy
    earlier in this chapter. Ponder which ones you can do
    at your state in life. Even if you are unable to go out to
    minister to someone, you can pray for others (the living
    and the dead). You can also bear wrongs patiently and
    forgive offences willingly.

2. Consider your use of time. Is some of it wasted? Is there
    time in your schedule you could devote in service to the
    poor in some way by cutting out (giving up) something
    you like to do? That would make it a bit more penitential
    and very possibly efficacious as well.

3. In what ways are you an example to others in service
    to the poor or unfortunate? Can you think of ways you
    could be a better example?

Seeking God

Dear Lord, Jesus, you are ever loving and merciful. Please teach
me to be more like you. Love through me, Lord, and open my
heart to those in need. I wish to bring others closer to you. Amen.

PART FIVE

*C*HRIST IS MY JOY

As the Father has loved me, so I have loved you;
abide in my love. If you keep my commandments, you will abide in my love. . . . I have said
these things to you so that my joy may be in you,
and that your joy may be complete.

—John 15:9–11

10. *My* Soul
Magnifies the Lord

> Let us run to Mary, and, as her little chil-
> dren, cast ourselves into her arms with a
> perfect confidence.
>
> —St. Francis de Sales

I remember well how my mother would call her brood together to kneel before a statue of the Blessed Mother to pray the family Rosary. A little votive candle flickered in blue glass before it. The memory is etched on my heart. She was the one in the family who carried out the responsibility of laying down a foundation of faith for us eight kids. Lest you think we all knelt reverently, hands clasped with sparkling halos hovering over our heads, think again! I'll be the first to tell you, we were never perfectly behaved. But we knelt and prayed the Rosary as a family on certain holy days and sometimes throughout the week. Mary might have been smiling at us, especially at my mother who fostered this ancient prayer devotion within her humble domestic church.

Because of my mother's example, I still have a love for the Rosary today. It has followed me through life, sometimes mysteriously showing up at times I would least expect. I have no doubt that Mother Mary always kept an eye on me, drawing me back to her whenever I lost my way. And so the Rosary, with Mary's help and God's grace, made its way into my own domestic church.

My maternal grandmother, Alexandra Uzwiak, also fostered devotion to the Rosary in my heart simply because of her example. This was more powerful than if she had told me about its wonderful benefits. I could clearly see her love for Mary in the sparkle of her eyes and in her tender smile while she quietly prayed.

The *Catechism* tells us,

> "The Church's devotion to the Blessed Virgin is intrinsic to Christian worship." The Church rightly honors the Blessed Virgin with special devotion. From the most ancient times the Blessed Virgin has been honored with the title of "Mother of God," to whose protection the faithful fly in all their dangers and needs. . . . This very special devotion . . . differs essentially from the adoration which is given to the incarnate Word and equally to the Father and the Holy Spirit, and greatly fosters this adoration. The liturgical feasts dedicated to the Mother of God and Marian prayer, such as the Rosary, an "epitome of the whole Gospel," express this devotion to the Virgin Mary. (CCC 971)

Through the ages Mary has become known by hundreds of titles. Some are biblical, like Mother of Jesus; some are due to the geographical location of her apparitions, like Our Lady of Lourdes. Some are titles of love and veneration and include Star of the Sea, Mediatrix, and Queen of Heaven. There are of course many more. But how much do we really know about Mary, the Mother of God? She says little in the scriptures, yet the Savior of the world was born through her. Her greatness on Earth was known to God even as she was clothed with profound humility. Amazingly, through Mary's humility and love, our Lord Jesus Christ was born into this world.

We know that Mary was a virgin. Preserved from original sin from the moment of her conception, she remained pure and sinless throughout her life. Pope Pius IX said, "The Most Blessed Virgin Mary was, from the first moment of her conception, by a singular grace and privilege of almighty God and by virtue of the merits of Jesus Christ, Savior of the human race, preserved immune from all stain of original sin."[1]

We also know that from all eternity God chose a daughter of Israel, a young Jewish teen of Nazareth in Galilee, to be the Mother of his Son. Throughout the Old Covenant many holy women prepared for the mission of Mary. First was Eve who, although disobedient, was promised a posterity that would be victorious over the evil one and that she would be the mother of all the living. Sarah, Hannah, Deborah, Ruth, Judith, and Esther, as well as many others, are noted in the Bible as women who were considered weak in some way but, through their faithfulness, fulfilled God's will in miraculous ways. Then enters Mary, through whom the new plan of salvation is established.

Even as a young Jewish girl, Mary prayed with a steadfast faith for the coming of the Messiah. Mary would have known of Isaiah's prophecy that a virgin would conceive and bear a child and name him Emmanuel (God with us). And though she believed that "nothing will be impossible with God" (Lk 1:37), as she prayed for the Messiah she didn't have a clue that *she* would be the one to bear the child! But the Holy Spirit prepared Mary's womb and prepared Mary's heart and soul with grace.

At the moment of the annunciation, the angel Gabriel saluted Mary as "full of grace." Mary then offered her whole being to God—her *fiat* (a Latin word that means "Let it be done"). She says, "Here am I, the servant of the Lord; let it be with me according to your word" (Lk 1:38). "Wholeheartedly, without a single sin to restrain her, she gave herself entirely to the person and to the work of her Son; she did so in order to serve the mystery of redemption with him and dependent on him, by God's grace" (LG 56).

Through her selfless *fiat*, Mary was collaborating with the entire work of what Jesus would accomplish. Through the Holy Spirit, Mary conceived and gave birth to Jesus, the Son of God. And the Word was made flesh (Lk 1:26–38). St. Irenaeus said,

> Being obedient she became the cause of salvation for herself and for the whole human race. . . . The knot of Eve's disobedience was united by Mary's obedience; what the virgin Eve bound through disbelief, Mary loosened by her faith. (CCC 494)

Mary is a great example of humility. The scriptures tell us that, through Mary, the Holy Spirit continues to bring humble people to God's merciful love through Jesus. We see that the first to accept Jesus as the Word made flesh were humble people: simple shepherds, the magi, Simeon and Anna in the Temple, the bride and groom at Cana, and the first disciples.

Blessed Mother Teresa remarked that, when the angel announced the coming of Christ to Mary, "Her lips uttered a beautiful response that asserted all that she was as a woman: 'I am the servant of the Lord. Let it be done to me as you say.'"[2]

Mary experienced the multifaceted joys of motherhood as she raised her Son in the blessedness of her humble home

along with St. Joseph. We can imagine the child Jesus on
Mary's lap and in her arms as she smothered him with motherly love. Like all babies, Jesus might have suffered from dia-
per rash on occasion, had tummy aches, or skinned his knees
when playing outside. Mary was thoroughly involved with
his care as mothers are. No doubt, Mary encouraged Jesus to
help St. Joseph with his carpentry as Jesus was growing up.
The close-knit Holy Family grew closer each day in divine
love.

MARY, OUR MOTHER

Mary was indeed a faithful woman—she remained faithful
to the care of her family as well as totally faithful to her Son's
mission, persevering through all the struggles and sorrow—
all the way to the Cross. After Jesus' three-year public life
and ministry, he was falsely accused, sold for thirty pieces
of silver, scourged, spat upon, beaten mercilessly, mocked,
crowned with thorns, and nailed to a wooden cross.

As Jesus hung diminishing on the cross, he called down
to his disciple John, "Behold, your mother!" He was also
speaking to all of his disciples down through until the end
of time, telling us all that his own Mother Mary had become
our mother. He gave us the gift of a loving mother totally
attuned to the thoughts of God and completely imbued with
the Word of God—full of love for us. Mary then became
the "new Eve" or mother of the living. Can we possibly
imagine this mother's sorrow as she watched and suffered
along with her Son at the foot of the cross? She is a mother
who knows deep suffering and certainly understands our
struggles and pain, too.

Mary was a prayerful woman. Her steadfast and faithful prayers aided the beginnings of the Church. After Jesus
had risen from the dead and ascended to heaven, Mary was

present with the twelve apostles who prayed together in the upper room for the coming of the Holy Spirit, whom Jesus had promised and who had already overshadowed Mary in the annunciation. St. Luke explained in the Acts of the Apostles, "All these were constantly devoting themselves to prayer, together with certain women, including Mary the mother of Jesus, as well as his brothers" (Acts 1:14).

Believers all over the world call upon the Blessed Mother for her help and motherly guidance. Pope Benedict XVI explained,

> Mary has truly become the Mother of all believers. Men and women of every time and place have recourse to her motherly kindness and her virginal purity and grace, in all their needs and aspirations, their joys and sorrows, their moments of loneliness and their common endeavors. They constantly experience the gift of her goodness and the unfailing love which she pours out from the depths of her heart. (*DCE* 42)

Let's not be afraid to approach Mary with anything. She awaits our greetings and conversations with her.

St. Bonaventure has said that all the angels in heaven cry out to her incessantly, "Holy, holy, holy Mary, Mother of God and Virgin." The angels offer her millions upon millions of the angelical salutation, the Ave Maria, each day while prostrating themselves before her. They beg her to honor them with some of her commands. St. Augustine said that even St. Michael, who is the prince of the heavenly court, is the most zealous in honoring Mary, always eagerly awaiting the honor of her biddings to go and help her servants. Imagine that!

Among Christians, Mary is revered as protectress for many provinces, kingdoms, dioceses, and cities. Every Catholic church, basilica, or chapel has an altar of honor for

Mary. Confraternities, congregations, and religious orders are founded in her name, and cathedrals are consecrated to God under her name. And our Church has designated many feast days in Mary's honor.

Numerous saints have been deeply devoted to Mary, including many popes. From Sixtus IV in 1479, to the present day, the popes have urged the faithful to pray the Rosary and have enriched it with indulgences. I have witnessed a modern-day saint, Blessed Mother Teresa, praying to Mary. She would pray the Rosary constantly. She also prayed the Memorare prayer as a novena by praying it nine times in a row for an urgent need and then nine times in thanksgiving for prayers answered, no matter what. Mother Teresa kept close company with our Blessed Mother.

St. Louis de Montfort, who was a strong devotee of Mary and promoter of the total consecration to Jesus through Mary, said,

> There is not a little child who, as it lisps the Hail Mary, does not praise her. There is scarcely a sinner who, even in his obduracy, has not some spark of confidence in her. Nay, the very devils in hell respect her while they fear her.[3]

Blessed John Paul II, who experienced a decisive turning point in his life when he read St. Louis de Montfort's words in his book *True Devotion to Mary*, said,

> At first, it seemed to me that I should distance myself a bit from the Marian devotion of my childhood in order to focus more on Christ. Thanks to St. Louis de Montfort, I came to understand that true devotion to the Mother of God is actually Christocentric; indeed, it is very profoundly rooted in the mystery of the Blessed Trinity, and the mysteries of the Incarnation and Redemption.[4]

Blessed John Paul II said he took his motto "Totus tuus" (I am all thine) from St. Louis de Montfort's teachings.

WHAT DOES MARY TELL US?

The Church reminds us of the Blessed Mother's role in our lives and encourages the faithful to commend their lives to her care in *Apostolicam Actuositatem* (*On the Apostolate of the Laity*).

> The perfect example of this type of spiritual and apostolic life is the most Blessed Virgin Mary, Queen of Apostles, who while leading the life common to all here on earth, one filled with family concerns and labors, was always intimately united with her Son and in an entirely unique way cooperated in the work of the Savior. Having now been assumed into heaven, with her maternal charity she cares for these brothers of her Son who are still on their earthly pilgrimage and remain involved in dangers and difficulties until they are led into the happy fatherland. All should devoutly venerate her and commend their life and apostolate to her maternal care. (*AA* 2)

Pope Benedict XVI speaks of the Blessed Mother's great holiness in *Deus Caritas Est*:

> Outstanding among the saints is Mary, Mother of the Lord and mirror of all holiness. In the *Gospel of Luke* we find her engaged in a service of charity to her cousin Elizabeth, with whom she remained for "about three months" (1:56) so as to assist her in the final phase of her pregnancy. (*DCE* 41)

When Mary was visited by the angel Gabriel, he told her that her elderly cousin Elizabeth was pregnant with John the Baptist. Rather than worry about her own pregnancy discomforts, Mary focused on the service of another and ran in haste to help Elizabeth for the remainder of her pregnancy. When Mary arrived at Elizabeth's home, the two holy women embraced, and Elizabeth praised Mary for her faith. Mary humbly responded with her song of praise.

Blessed Teresa of Calcutta spoke about our Blessed Mother's generous heart in her loving service to Elizabeth:

> The wonderful tenderness of a woman's heart: to be aware of the sufferings of others and to try to spare them that suffering, as Mary did. Do you and I have that same tenderness in our hearts? Do we have Mary's eyes for discovering the needs of others?[5]

Perhaps we can take some time to ponder how God might be calling us to "run in haste" to aid someone. Could it be our spouse, our child, our fellow nun, our coworker, or our lonely neighbor?

Mary's joyful response to her cousin Elizabeth's greeting (Lk 1:41–45) is recorded in the Gospel of Luke (1:46–55). It's really the longest discourse recorded of Mary in divine revelation. Through Mary's song of praise and adoration, now left to us, we can all learn to thank and praise God as Mary did. It's a prayer of humble adoration, a most important form of prayer.

Blessed John Paul II reminds us in *Redemptoris Mater* (*Mother of the Redeemer*) about Mary's humble mission of service:

> She who at the Annunciation called herself the "handmaid of the Lord" remained throughout her earthly life faithful to what this name expresses. In this she confirmed that she was a true "disciple" of Christ, who

strongly emphasized that his mission was one of service: the Son of man "came not to be served but to serve,
and to give his life as a ransom for many" (Mt 20:28).
In this way, Mary became the first of those who "serving Christ also in others, with humility and patience
led her brothers and sisters to that King whom to serve
is to reign," and she fully obtained that "state of royal
freedom" proper to Christ's disciples: to serve means
to reign! (*RM* 41)

God is calling us all to a mission of loving, selfless service. Not to compare myself in any way to Jesus or Mary,
but there has not been a single time when I practiced charity toward someone that I have not come away from it with
much more than I could have possibly given. "To serve
means to reign!"

The Magnificat has been prayed and sung since the ear-
liest of centuries by monks, hermits, and religious consecrated to God. It's been put to music by composers such as
Palestrina, Bach, and Mozart. In our day, many pray this
prayer of thanks and praise as part of their evening prayers,
which is part of the Church's Liturgy of the Hours. I think
as we pray her song of praise we should remember that,
when Mary first proclaimed it, our Lord Jesus was present
in her womb, the first tabernacle. What an intensely holy
song of praise!

The two blessed women, both expecting, must have
enjoyed glorious times in Elizabeth's modest home as they
relished in their blessed pregnancies together. I imagine
that, even though Mary was there specifically to lend her
heart and hands to Elizabeth, she must have also benefited
from Elizabeth's tender love and company. It reminds me of
the companionship and love we too experience as Catholic
women reaching out to help one another.

The *Catechism* calls the Magnificat or Canticle of Mary

the song both of the Mother of God and of the Church;
the song of the Daughter of Zion and the new People of
God; the song of thanksgiving for the fullness of graces
poured out in the economy of salvation and the song of
the "poor" whose hope is met by the fulfillment of the
promises made to our ancestors, "to Abraham and to his
posterity for ever." (CCC 2619)

THE MAGNIFICAT

My soul magnifies the Lord
And my spirit rejoices in God my Savior;
Because he has regarded the lowliness of his
    handmaid;
For behold, henceforth all generations shall call me
    blessed;
Because he who is mighty has done great things for
    me,
and holy is his name;
And his mercy is from generation to generation
on those who fear him.
He has shown might with his arm,
He has scattered the proud in the conceit of their
    heart.
He has put down the mighty from their thrones,
and has exalted the lowly.
He has filled the hungry with good things,
and the rich he has sent away empty.
He has given help to Israel, his servant, mindful of his
    mercy
Even as he spoke to our fathers, to Abraham and to his
    posterity forever.

Through her song of praise and adoration, Mary tells us that God's mercy is boundless for the weak and fallen and that God always keeps his promises. Throughout history humankind has failed God miserably, yet God does not fail us. He will not abandon us.

Let's take St. Ambrose's advice: "Let Mary's soul be in us to glorify the Lord; let her spirit be in us that we may rejoice in God our Savior."

In addition to the many titles of Mary, there are numerous images of her illustrated in paintings, icons, art, statues, and the like. Many depict Mary with baby Jesus on her lap or in her arms. Some are of her standing alone, arms outstretched, or holding the Rosary. Numerous images of Mary crushing the head of the serpent abound, showing her power over the wiles and wickedness of the devil. We should always feel free to call upon Mother Mary at any time for help and protection. She is powerful over evil.

We are blessed that Blessed Mother Mary was sent to our world in many apparitions throughout the ages. She was sent from heaven for many major reasons, including to urge the faithful to pray to hold off a war; to instruct us to pray for sinners and the souls in purgatory; to appeal to the faithful for penance and prayer, especially the prayer of the Rosary; and so on. Millions of pilgrims have traveled to the places of Mary's apparitions including to Fatima, Portugal; Lourdes, France; Guadalupe, Mexico; and Champion, Wisconsin (near Green Bay), to experience healings in their bodies, minds, and souls.

How We Can Emulate Mary

How can I as a Catholic woman emulate the virtues, holiness, and goodness of Mary? Or can I? Can I approach the Mother of God? We might feel it's impossible to reach her.

After all, she's in heaven. Or we might fear approaching her since we are imperfect. Let's consider her humanness for a moment. Mary was no stranger to the many difficulties of life and the great sorrows—she thoroughly understood them.

When we Catholic women experience uncertainties and doubt, perhaps we can think of Mary's life. Her mode of transportation was not convenient (a donkey!) and of course not as luxurious as ours. As St. Joseph and Mary searched for a place to give birth to their unborn Child, pregnant Mary was jostled around on the back of an animal. Our Blessed Mother clearly understands the pain of rejection, having been turned away from a suitable place to give birth. And Mary knows the pain of being uprooted when she and Joseph had to flee with Jesus to Egypt to escape Herod's plan to kill him.

Later on, Mary felt the pain of her Son being abandoned by the people he helped. And Mary stood at the foot of the cross as her own Son gasped his last breath and bled from his five wounds out of divine love for all of us. She deeply grieved as she held his lifeless body in her arms when he was taken down from the Cross. She thoroughly knew suffering.

Mary's prayers were pure, faithful, and efficacious. St. John tells us that Mary observed a bride and groom would not have enough wine for their wedding guests and, wanting to help, informed Jesus. "They have no wine." Jesus told her that his hour had not come yet. So, Mary simply and with prayerful confidence instructed the wine stewards to "do whatever he tells you" (Jn 2:2–11). Her prayerful obedience, by God's grace, prodded her Son to work his first public miracle.

Sometimes we might find it difficult to trust God. We can learn from Mary and meditate on her faith in God as

one who allowed the Holy Spirit to guide and inspire her as
she gave herself completely to the will of the Father. We'll
certainly never compare to Mary, by a long shot, but we can
also surrender our wills to God with his grace.

Busy women might feel it's impossible to find silence in
their lives in which to retreat to their hearts to pray. Blessed
Mother Teresa said, "Mary can teach us silence—how to
keep all things in our hearts as she did, to pray in the silence
of our hearts." Let's ask Mary to guide us to discover the
essential silence we absolutely need.

Blessed Mother Teresa also taught,

> Mary will teach us humility—though full of grace yet
> only a handmaid of the Lord, she stands as one of us at
> the foot of the cross, a sinner needing redemption. Let
> us, like her, touch the dying, the poor, the lonely, and the
> unwanted according to the graces we have received, and
> let us not be ashamed or slow to do the humble work.[6]

And so we ponder: *if Mary who was the Mother of God
was also his handmaid and delighted to serve others, how can I
be a handmaid, too?* We discussed various ways we Catholic
women serve others in earlier chapters. Let us now consider
becoming a "servant of the Lord" with Mary's help and
grace.

Mary is our refuge. Let us not be afraid of turning to
Mary and asking for her help in overcoming a vice, sin, or
problem. Servant of God Archbishop Fulton Sheen said,

> Mary is a refuge of sinners. She who is Virgin Most Pure
> is also the Refuge of Sinners. She knows what sin is,
> not by the experience of its falls, not by tasting its bitter
> regrets, but by seeing what it did to her divine Son.[7]

In his book *Introduction to the Devout Life,* St. Francis de
Sales encourages us to approach Mary often with honor and
with a childlike love and abandon:

> Honor and revere with a special love the blessed and
> glorious Virgin Mary. She is the Mother of God our
> Father, and she is also our Mother. Let us, therefore,
> have recourse to her, and, like little children, let us cast
> ourselves into her arms with a perfect confidence. Let
> us call upon this sweet Mother, invoking her maternal
> love, attempting to imitate her virtues and having a filial
> heart in her regard.[8]

St. Louis de Montfort prods us on. We must cry out with
the saints,

> *"De Maria numquam satis"*—"Of Mary there is never
> enough." We have not yet praised, exalted, honored,
> loved and served Mary as we ought. She deserves still
> more praise, still more respect, still more love, and still
> more service.[9]

Holy Mother Church encourages us to pray with and to
Mary. We read in the Catechism,

> Mary is the perfect Orans (pray-er), a figure of the
> Church. When we pray to her, we are adhering with
> her to the plan of the Father, who sends his Son to save
> all men. Like the beloved disciple we welcome Jesus'
> mother into our homes, for she has become the mother
> of all the living. We can pray with and to her. The prayer
> of the Church is sustained by the prayer of Mary and
> united with it in hope. (*CCC* 2679)

There are numerous prayers to Mary including the
ancient prayer of the Rosary, the Hail Mary, the Memorare,
the Angelus, the Regina Coeli, the total consecration to Jesus

through Mary as taught by St. Louis de Montfort, litanies, scores of novena prayers, and more. As Catholic women, we are certainly not expected to pray them all! But we should take some time to discover what sort of Marian prayer is fitting for us.

Personally, I love the Rosary because of its beauty and meaning and also because I know that Mary loves it. I want to make her happy, so I pray it, and each day I try to make time to fit it into my schedule. I tell you this so you won't dismiss the Rosary as a possibility for your own prayer life, just because you fear you don't have the time. Sometimes, we just have to force ourselves to pray even when we are rushed for time. It's when we need it most really. Many times my Rosary is broken up into decades, which are spread throughout the day, since at this point in my life I can rarely sit or kneel long enough to complete praying an entire Rosary at once.

I enjoy speaking to Mary often. Your prayers to Mary don't have to be complicated or in any special formula—just start talking with her. Give her the praise and honor she deserves. Blessed Mother Teresa taught me a simple but poignant prayer to Mary that I'll never forget. "Mary, Mother of Jesus, make me alright; Mary, Mother of Jesus, be a Mother to me now." I say that prayer often, and I teach it to others.

I sometimes imagine being with Mother Mary and cuddling up close to her, near her Immaculate Heart when I pray to her, especially when I really need her help or when I have trouble sleeping. One time when my friend and colleague Lisa was traveling out of state to give a presentation, she told me she feared she wouldn't get very good sleep away from home since she was just getting over an illness and that the travel might do her in. I told her I'd pray for her and would ask the Blessed Mother to take care of her needs. I added, "Just lie on Mary's heart." Upon returning from her

trip, Lisa told me that she had the most amazing, energiz-
ing, and grace-filled trip and that she slept like a baby each
night after prayerfully "laying her head on Mary's heart."
Mary is the most wonderful Mother of all! Let's all lean our
heads on Mary's heart often.

To Jesus through Mary!

A MOMENT TO REFLECT

The Blessed Mother has so much to teach us. She wants to
be our Mother. We can endeavor to get closer to her through
our prayers and time spent with her in conversation. We
should learn more about her through solid spiritual reading. I recommend St. Louis de Montfort's writings as well
as anything from our popes. Encyclicals and other Church
documents can be found on the Vatican's website. Some
helpful ones regarding Mary are *Ineffabilis Deus*, *Ad Diem
Illum Laetissimum*, *Ad Caeli Reginam*, *Lumen Gentium* (chapter
8), *Redemptoris Mater*, *Virginis Mariae*, *Mulieris Dignitatem*,
Rosarium Virginis Mariae, and so many of Blessed John Paul
II's General Audiences.

When Mary appeared to St. Juan Diego in Guadalupe,
Mexico, she reassured him, "Am I not here, I, who am your
Mother? Are you not under my shadow and protection? Am
I not the source of your joy? Are you not in the hollow of my
mantle, in the crossing of my arms? Do you need anything
more? Let nothing else worry you, disturb you."

Let's put ourselves under Mary's protection, safe within
the "hollow" of her mantle. With a childlike abandon, "let
us run to Mary, and, as her little children, cast ourselves into
her arms with a perfect confidence" (St. Francis de Sales).

My Mind to Know Him

1. During the course of your day, do you think about the Blessed Mother?

2. Can you take some time to learn more about Mary through Church documents and writings of the saints?

3. Have you endeavored to teach others in some way about Mary? Can you think about how you might be able to do so, according to your state in life?

My Heart to Love Him

1. Do you pray to the Blessed Mother and ask her to bring you closer to her Son?

2. Have you prayed the Rosary? Can you try to fit even one decade into your schedule each day?

3. If you are a mother or grandmother, are you fostering a devotion to the Blessed Mother among your children or grandchildren with your example and your spoken word?

My Hands to Serve Him

1. Throughout your acts of service to someone, ask the Blessed Mother to aid you and the recipient in some way that is pleasing to God.

2. Is there some sort of undertaking you might be able to get involved in at your parish or in your community that would bring honor to the Blessed Mother?

3. Can you list three ideas of how you might lend a hand to someone in your life in imitation of our Blessed Mother's mission of service?

A Prayer to Mary

As I pray my Rosary and show you my love, dear Mary, allow my *mind* to meditate on the holy mysteries, my *heart* to pray deeply, and my *hands* to hold my blessed beads. Grant me the graces through my rosaries and prayers to you and with you to extend my hands to others in need. Please ask your Son Jesus to grant me the courage and love to whole-heartedly offer myself as a "servant of the Lord."

> Holy Mary, Mother of God, our Mother, teach us to believe, to hope, to love with you. Show us the way to his Kingdom! Star of the Sea, shine upon us and guide us on our way! (*SS* 50)

A Prayer of Thanksgiving to Our Lord

Thank you, dear Lord, for the incredible gift of being a Catholic woman. Please open and inspire my mind to learn more about my faith; please fill my heart with the fire of your love so I will be open to your graces and blessings; and please give strength to my hands so I may continually serve you in others each day of my life. Amen.

Jesus, I love you! Jesus, I trust in You!

A FINAL WORD

Thank you for joining me in this "slumber party" while dis-
covering your feminine genius and true calling as a Catholic
woman. Be sure to celebrate your feminine holiness in all
that you do, being a Christian model for all. Live your life
brimming with faith, hope, and love which will indeed help
to guide and light the way for others. And, let's remember
St. Clare of Assisi's simple instructions, "Love God, serve
God: everything is in that."

May God richly bless you!

> The Church gives thanks for all the manifestations of the
> feminine "genius" which have appeared in the course
> of history, in the midst of all peoples and nations; she
> gives thanks for all the charisms which the Holy Spirit
> distributes to women in the history of the People of God,
> for all the victories which she owes to their faith, hope
> and charity; she gives thanks for all the fruits of feminine
> holiness. (*MD* 31)

ABBREVIATIONS

AA   *On the Apostolate of the Laity (Apostolicam Actuositatem)*. Vatican Council II, 1965.

DCE   *God Is Love (Deus Caritas Est)*. Encyclical Letter of Benedict XVI, 2005.

FC   *The Role of the Christian Family in the Modern World (Familiaris Consortio)*. Apostolic Exhortation of John Paul II, 1981.

GS   *Pastoral Constitution on the Church in the Modern World (Gaudium et Spes)*. Vatican Council II, 1965.

HV   *On Human Life (Humane Vitae)*. Encyclical Letter of Paul VI, 1968.

LG   *Dogmatic Constitution on the Church (Lumen Gentium)*. Vatican Council II, 1964.

MD   *On the Dignity and Vocation of Women (Mulieris Dignitatem)*. Apostolic Letter of John Paul II, 1988.

RM   *The Mother of the Redeemer (Redemptoris Mater)*. Encyclical Letter of John Paul II, 1987.

SS   *Saved in Hope (Spe Salvi)*. Encyclical Letter of Benedict XVI, 2007.

VD   *The Word of the Lord (Verbum Domini)*. Post-Synodal Apostolic Exhortation of Benedict XVI, 2010.

NOTES

INTRODUCTION

1. Léopold (de Chérancé), *St. Clare of Assisi*, translated by Robert Francis O'Connor (London: Birns & Oates, 1927) 198.

1. WHO AM I?

1. John Paul II, *Letter to Women*, June 29, 1995, http://www.vatican.va.

2. Gregory Joseph Ladd, *Fulton J. Sheen: A Man for All Media* (San Francisco: Ignatius Press, 2001), 123.

3. St. Thérèse of Lisieux, *The Story of a Soul*, translated by John Beevers (New York: Image, 1987).

2. BECOMING A WHOLE WOMAN

1. John A. Hardon, *Modern Catholic Dictionary* (Bardstown, KY: Eternal Life, 2000).

2. John A. Hardon, "The Sacraments of Baptism and Confirmation," Catholic Education Resource Center, 1998, http://www.catholiceducation.org.

3. Hardon, "The Sacraments of Baptism and Confirmation."

4. Ronda De Sola Chervin, *Quotable Saints* (Ann Arbor, MI: Servant Publications, 1992).

5. Josemaria Escrivá, *Furrow* (New York: Scepter, 1987), 514.

4. OFFERING ME LIVING WATER

1. *De orat.* 12: Patrologia Graeca 11, 452C.

2. Mental Prayer, Parochial and Plain Sermons VII, 205–6, December 13, 1829.

3. John A. Hardon, *Theology of Prayer* (Boston: Daughters of St. Paul, 1979).

4. St. Teresa of Avila, *The Book of Her Life*, 8, 5, in *The Collected Works of St. Teresa of Avila*, trans. K. Kavanaugh, O.C.D., and O. Rodriguez, O.C.D. (Washington, DC: Institute of Carmelite Studies, 1976), I:67.

5. St. Peter Julian Eymard, *A Eucharistic Handbook* (Cleveland, OH: Emmanuel Publications, n.d.).

6. Hardon, *Theology of Prayer*, 136.

7. Eymard, *Eucharistic Handbook*.

8. Benedict XVI, *Verbum Domini*, September 30, 2010, http://www.vatican.va/.

9. A nice explanation of Lectio Divina can be found at Fish Eaters, http://www.fisheaters.com/lectiodivina.html.

10. For helpful information about the devotion to the Sacred Heart of Jesus and the Immaculate Heart of Mary as well as devotional prayers, see EWTN's website at http://www.ewtn.com/devotionals/heart/index.htm.

11. The EWTN website has some great information on the Rosary: http://www.ewtn.com/devotionals/prayers/rosary.

12. Mara Faustina Kowalska, *Diary: Divine Mercy in My Soul* (Stockbridge, MA: Marian Press, 2003) 47.

13. Ibid., 848.

14. Ibid., 300.

15. Learn more about this devotion from the Congregation of Marians of the Immaculate Conception of the Most Blessed Virgin Mary, http://www.marian.org/; and "Background of the Divine Mercy Devotion," EWTN, accessed May 8, 2012, http://www.ewtn.com/devotionals/mercy/backgr.htm.

16. Hardon, 19, *Theology of Prayer or which is it?*

17. Ibid., 19–20.

18. Ibid.

19. St. Francis de Sales, *Introduction to the Devout Life: A Popular Abridgment* (Charlotte, NC: Saint Benedict Press, 1990), 8.

20. Chervin, *Quotable Saints*, 116.

5. In My Home

1. Pius XII, Address to Italian Women, October 21, 1945, *Acta Apostolicae Sedis* 37 (1945), 287.

2. Joan Lewis, *Joan's Rome* (blog), http://www.ewtn.com/news/blog.asp?blog_id=1; to hear a sample of her EWTN television spot, see "Joan's Rome: Pope's Wednesday Audience," YouTube, updated August 26, 2010, http://www.youtube.com/watch?v=N9ObwYWkoE8.

3. Teresa of Avila, *The Complete Works of St. Teresa of Jesus*, vol. 1, *General Introduction, Life, Spiritual Relations*, trans. E. Allison Peers (New York: Sheed and Ward, 1972), 19.

6. In My Work

1. Escrivá, *Furrow*, 803.

2. Michael E. Gaitley, M.I.C., *Consoling the Heart of Jesus: Prayer Companion* (Stockbridge, MA: Marian Press, 2010), 69.

7. In My Struggles

1. Jean-Pierre de Caussade, *Abandonment to Divine Providence* (New York: Doubleday, 1975), 50.

2. Homily given on January 5, 2008, the memorial of St. John Neumann, at a Mass commemorating the seventh anniversary of the death of Father John A. Hardon, S.J., founder of the Marian Catechist Apostolate, on the occasion of the Apostolate's day of reflection at the Shrine of Our Lady of Guadalupe in La Crosse, Wisconsin.

3. Father John A. Hardon, S.J., "Christ Speaks to Us: Words from One of Our Spiritual Fathers," Father John A. Hardon, S.J., Archives: Education, Real Presence Association, http://www.therealpresence.org/archives/Education/Education_001.htm.

4. Father John A. Hardon, S.J., Archives Index, Real Presence Association, http://www.therealpresence.org/archives/archives.htm and http://godisatworkinyou.blogspot.com/2012/01/servant-of-god-fr-john-hardon-sj-on-neo.html.

5. *A Year with the Saints* (New York: P.J. Kennedy & Sons, 1891), 22.

8. A WOMAN FOR OTHERS

1. St. Francis de Sales, *Introduction to the Devout Life*, 54.
2. Escrivá, *Furrow*, 846.

9. WHEN DID I SEE YOU, LORD?

1. Kowalska, *Diary*, 1777.
2. Ibid., 1541.
3. Hardon, "Sacraments of Baptism and Confirmation."
4. Joseph P. Christopher, Charles E. Spence, and John F. Rowan, *The Raccolta* (Fitzwilliam, NH: Loreto Publications, 2004).

10. MY SOUL MAGNIFIES THE LORD

1. *Ineffabilis Deus*, 1854: Denzinger-Schönmetzer 2803.
2. From a talk Blessed Teresa of Calcutta gave at the Forty-First International Eucharistic Congress in Philadelphia, August 7, 1976.
3. St. Louis de Montfort, *True Devotion to Mary* (Chula Vista, CA: Aventine Press, 2007).
4. John Paul II, *Crossing the Threshold of Hope* (New York: Knopf, 1994), 212–13.
5. Mother Teresa of Calcutta, *Heart of Joy* (Ann Arbor, MI: Servant, 1987).
6. Susan Conroy, *Mother Teresa's Lessons of Love* (Huntington, IN: Our Sunday Visitor, 2003).
7. Fulton J. Sheen, *Victory over Vice* (New York: P. J. Kennedy and Sons, 1939), 39.
8. St. Francis de Sales, *Introduction to the Devout Life*, 90.
9. St. Louis de Montfort, *True Devotion to Mary*.

Donna-Marie Cooper O'Boyle is an award-winning author and journalist, speaker, reviewer, and the EWTN television host of *Everyday Blessings for Catholic Moms,* which she created. A Catholic wife and mother of five, Cooper O'Boyle was noted as one of the Top Ten Most Fascinating Catholics in 2009 by *Faith & Family Live.* She enjoyed a decade-long friendship with Blessed Mother Teresa of Calcutta and became a Lay Missionary of Charity. For many years her spiritual director was Servant of God John A. Hardon, S.J., who also served as one of Mother Teresa's spiritual directors.

Cooper O'Boyle was invited by the Holy See in 2008 to participate in an international congress for women at the Vatican to mark the twentieth anniversary of the apostolic letter *Mulieris Dignitatem (On the Dignity and Vocation of Women).* She received apostolic blessings from Blessed Pope John Paul II and Pope Benedict XVI on her books and work and a special blessing from Pope John Paul II for her work with Blessed Mother Teresa. Cooper O'Boyle is the author of several books on faith and family, including *Bringing Lent Home with Mother Teresa, Mother Teresa and Me, Embracing Motherhood,* and *The Domestic Church.* She has been featured by Zenit news and *Rome Reports,* and is a frequent guest on *EWTN Bookmark, Faith & Culture,* and *Vatican Insider.*

Founded in 1865, Ave Maria Press,
a ministry of the Congregation of
Holy Cross, is a Catholic publishing
company that serves the spiritual and
formative needs of the Church and its
schools, institutions, and ministers;
Christian individuals and families; and
others seeking spiritual nourishment.

For a complete listing of titles from

Ave Maria Press

Sorin Books

Forest of Peace

Christian Classics

visit www.avemariapress.com

ave maria press® / Notre Dame, IN 46556
A Ministry of the United States Province of Holy Cross

Pat - Rip - 9/21